Foreword

With the encouragement of the Home Office, selected probation areas set up and developed experimental intensive probation (IP) programmes to run for two years from April 1990. IP was targeted primarily at young adult offenders, a group responsible for a great deal of crime; it aimed to divert such offenders from custody by providing a rigorous and demanding community penalty which would utilise a multi-agency approach. The study reported on here monitored all referrals to IP programmes, and investigated three programmes in detail.

The findings suggest that, overall, IP was successful in its targeting. Variations in programmes and the way in which they were implemented, however, were significant factors in the development of IP. These issues are often ignored in policy planning and it is hoped that this research will help to draw attention to them. A future report will look at the reconviction rates associated with intensive probation.

ROGER TARLING
Head of Research and Planning Unit

July 1994

HOME OFFICE RESEARCH STUDY No.133

Intensive Probation in England and Wales: An evaluation

by George Mair, Charles Lloyd, Claire Nee and Rae Sibbitt

A HOME OFFICE
RESEARCH AND PLANNING UNIT
REPORT

LONDON: HMSO

ISBN 0 11 341114 6

HOME OFFICE RESEARCH STUDIES

'Home Office Research Studies' comprise reports on research undertaken in the Home Office to assist in the exercise of its administrative functions, and for the information of the judicature, the services for which the Home Secretary has responsibility (direct or indirect) and the general public.

On the last pages of this report are listed titles already published in this series, in the preceding series *Studies in the Causes of Delinquency and the Treatment of Offenders,* and in the series of *Research and Planning Unit Papers.*

HMSO

Standing Order Service

Placing a standing order with HMSO BOOKS enables a customer to receive other titles in this series automatically as published.

This saves time, trouble and the expense of placing individual orders and avoids the problems of knowing when to do so.

For details please write to HMSO BOOKS (PC11B.2), Publications Centre, P.O. Box 276, London SW8 5DT and quoting reference 25.08.011.

The standing order service also enables customers to receive automatically as published all material of their choice which additionally saves extensive catalogue research. The scope and selectivity of the service has been extended by new techniques, and there are more than 3,500 classifications to choose from. A special leaflet describing the service in more detail may be obtained on request.

Acknowledgements

A study of this scope would not have been possible without the co-operation and support of a great many individuals. We are grateful to all those members of the probation service who completed (and continue to complete) the monitoring forms, and to all those who discussed IP with us. Magistrates, judges and offenders provided us with their views and we also wish to thank them for all their help.

More specifically, for the three case studies we wish to thank John Burns, Christine Morgan and Steve Johnson in Durham; Paul Thurston, Terry Myers and Steve Lawrenson in Leeds; and David Hancock and Richard Marsh in the West Midlands for their co-operation and support. Sharon Jowitt helped with the coding of the data, and Mike Hough's comments on an early draft of the report were as helpful as ever.

GEORGE MAIR
CHARLES LLOYD
CLAIRE NEE
RAE SIBBITT

Contents

Summary

The intensive probation (IP) initiative grew out of concern about the level of crime among 17-20 year olds and the need to develop appropriate sentences for this age group, short of imprisonment. Early in 1989, selected probation areas were invited by the Home Office to establish IP programmes; these were planned to run for two years from April 1990. The Home Office Research and Planning Unit set up a study to examine the operation and impact of the initiative. This report focuses on its operation, covering only part of the impact; a further study will examine reconviction rates.

The main findings of the research were:

- Offenders were generally positive about IP and felt it had prevented them re-offending.
- The quality of organisation and management seemed at least as important a determinant of success as the precise nature of the scheme.
- 1,677 offenders were considered as candidates for, or sentenced to, IP between 1 April 1990 and 31 March 1992. Forty five per cent of these were sentenced to IP.
- Offenders serving IP orders generally had long criminal histories, and most had already served a custodial sentence.
- Two thirds of referrals who were not sentenced to IP were given a custodial disposal.
- Though all eight schemes carried the 'Intensive Probation' label, there was little commonality between the schemes and not all followed Home Office guidelines.

Background

Thoughts on IP were first mooted in the Green Paper *Punishment, Custody and the Community* and were further developed in the discussion document *Tackling Offending: an action plan.* IP schemes were expected to provide an alternative to custody for offenders considered likely to receive a custodial sentence. The target group was offenders between 17 and 25 years old who had been charged with fairly serious offences such as burglary.

An IP order was to consist of an individualised programme based on a personal action plan drawn up for the offender, and had to include arrangements for frequent contact between a project worker and the offender. Projects were expected to operate rigorous referral and selection procedures, to focus on confronting offending behaviour and to use a multi-agency approach; in addition, they were expected to ensure provision for female and ethnic minority offenders.

Of the ten probation services invited to participate, eight agreed to set up IP schemes in accordance with Home Office guidelines. Of those eight, one closed down in April 1991 and took only 17 referrals ('referrals' is used to cover offenders who were either referred for assessment to IP schemes, recommended for IP in a social inquiry report or sentenced to IP). There was considerable variation in the way the services interpreted IP, in terms of the age range dealt with, the kind of projects set up and which courts were targeted.

A total of 1,677 referrals were made between April 1990 and March 1992. The large majority of these cases came within the intended age range (Figure 1).

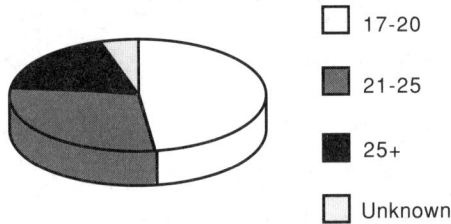

Figure 1. Age of referrals

Six per cent were non-white and only five per cent were female. A high proportion of the offences with which referrals were charged were serious, e.g. 42 per cent of main offences were burglary (see Figure 2).

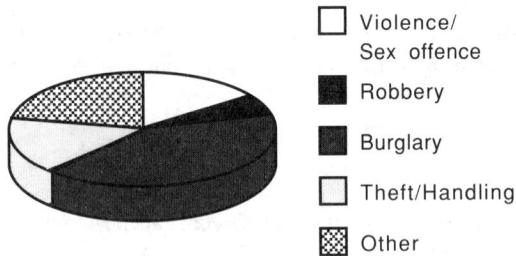

Figure 2. Main Offence

Only six per cent of referrals were first offenders and 51 per cent had six or more previous convictions (Figure 3); 54 per cent had served a previous custodial sentence. Sixty-four per cent of referrals were made via the Crown Court. At sentence, 45 per cent of those referred received IP and 37 per cent received custody.

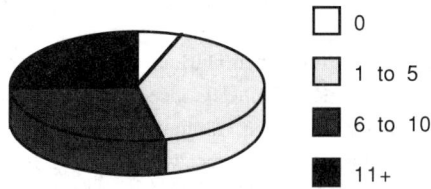

	0
	1 to 5
	6 to 10
	11+

Figure 3. Number of previous convictions

The disposal of referrals within the target age range is shown in Figure 4. Young adult offenders were more likely to be given IP than those aged 21 and over.

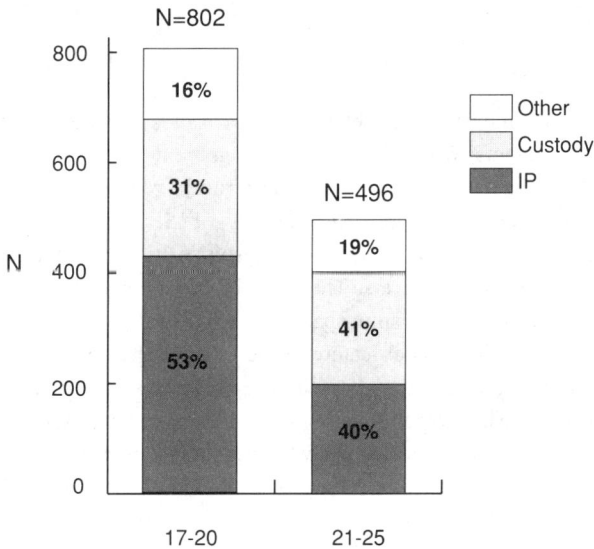

Figure 4. Disposal of IP referrals aged 17-25

Sentencers tended to be very positive about IP, although they had differing views about its objectives. Probation officers, especially those who worked on IP schemes, were also enthusiastic. Offenders appreciated the attention given to them by IP workers and thought they would be less likely to offend as a result of the IP scheme. Voluntary organisations were involved in all IP schemes to some extent, but there was unease amongst probation staff about making use of such groups.

Case studies were carried out in three probation areas: Durham, West Yorkshire (Leeds) and the West Midlands.

Durham

The IP initiative came at a time when Durham probation service was already considering a new alternative to custody scheme. Consequently, the GATE project, a partnership between the probation service and a voluntary body, was quickly set up. IP involved 60 contact days in all, contact with a project worker being frequent in the early stages and progressively decreasing. Work done on the order could consist of group work at a day centre (focusing on issues such as offending behaviour or alcohol education), individual counselling by project workers or constructive use of leisure time. Some activities were enforceable formal requirements of the order while others were voluntary (although sometimes voluntary activities were counted as contact days and so blurred this distinction).

Leeds

Leeds ran two IP programmes, one targeting 17-20 year olds and the other targeting 21-25 year olds. The projects differed in their management and in the content of the programme itself. The first – the Edge (which was run in partnership with a voluntary body) – started from scratch, whereas the second – LISP – evolved from previous 'tracking' schemes used in the area. Partly as a result of its origin, the latter was less readily accepted by maingrade officers. The Edge IP programme lasted 60 days while LISP consisted of 60 contacts over an unspecified period of time. The programmes also differed in their content. An essential feature of the LISP programme was that offenders were required to state their activities until the next contact so the programme worker could check up on them. Maingrade officers saw LISP as more controlling than the Edge. Both projects successfully targeted offenders who were at risk of custody.

West Midlands

In the West Midlands, IP was envisaged as an expanded version of a 4A programme (probation plus added requirements e.g. attendance at an alcohol education group) which would include input from voluntary organisations on accommodation, employment and leisure issues. It was also intended to be the sole high tariff probation order for the local target age group of 17-21 years. Senior management's motivation for setting up the IP programme was to improve the consistency of practice across teams and divisions on high tariff probation orders. Thus attempts were made to make existing 4A orders more consistent by requiring that the nature of the programme be specified more clearly in social inquiry reports. Teams were also encouraged to use a standard measurement of risk of custody in targeting IP and were requested to make formal consideration of voluntary agency input.

From the start, the exercise was greeted sceptically by maingrade officers in the West Midlands. They saw the whole process as essentially renaming an existing order and 'dressing it up' with a substantial amount of unnecessary paperwork. In addition, the input from voluntary organisations was not legally part of the order, and so attendance could not be enforced, reducing further the distinction between IP and the standard 4A order. Hostility towards the new practices was further fuelled by a perceived lack of clarity about what IP was and how it was to be targeted.

After two years, due mainly to opposition from field teams, the extra paperwork was abandoned, and soon after this the IP experiment was formally closed. While senior management considered that the initiative had been successful in terms of increasing consistency across divisions, it was also clear that the implementation of IP in the West Midlands had resulted in considerable confusion and loss of morale.

Conclusions

To conclude, the IP initiative resulted in a wide variety of schemes which, on the whole, successfully targeted high risk offenders. IP demonstrated, therefore, that probation services could develop rigorous programmes which dealt with such offenders. However, there were significant differences between the policy as developed centrally and some of the IP schemes which were put into practice. Not all areas were willing and/or able to follow Home Office guidelines, and indeed there were few signs of innovation in the IP schemes studied. No matter how well an initiative is conceived, effective and appropriate structures are needed to translate it into practice, and this was not always the case as far as IP was concerned.

IP was also important from a symbolic point of view. It can be read as one step amongst many in a campaign to move the probation service towards a more rigorous and demanding approach to dealing with offenders. In this respect IP was successful as even in those areas where there had been considerable scepticism about the initiative, attitudes did seem to change during the course of the experiment. As a vehicle for changing the working ethos of the probation service, intensive probation should not be under-estimated.

A follow-up study will investigate sentencing patterns in IP areas and will study the reconviction rate of offenders on intensive probation.

1 Introduction

During the course of the 1980s, intensive probation programmes in a bewildering variety of forms spread across probation services in the USA. Like many new developments in penal practice in the USA (the movement has not been one-way; community service and day centres are the most recent examples of British initiatives taken up in North America), the concept of intensive probation was incorporated onto the policy agenda in England and Wales and resulted in a series of experiments in several probation areas in 1990-1992.

Since its formal beginnings at the start of the twentieth century, the probation service has gone through many changes; theoretical approaches have come and gone, new practical applications have been developed, and administrative and bureaucratic structures have grown as the service has expanded in size and the scope of its work. In the 1980s, however, the probation service has had to cope with an unprecedented number of changes as a host of new initiatives have been developed and new policies have been devised. Simply to list some of the most important of these developments gives some idea of their significance: the Statement of National Objectives and Priorities, developmental work on a Resource Management Information System (initially a Financial Management Information System), the development and application of performance indicators, the widespread use of computers at all levels, the rapid growth of day centres (now renamed as probation centres) and specified activities programmes, the use of statistical prediction instruments, the introduction and national expansion of bail information schemes, the application of National Standards for community service (since October 1992, National Standards have been introduced for other aspects of mainstream probation work). This is an impressive list of developments (and they ignore the changes introduced by the Criminal Justice Act 1991), which have implications for the probation service beyond their immediate impact.

Although these developments can be seen as individual and discrete, their cumulative impact has been considerable. Overall, they have made the probation service more accountable for what it does and more controlling in how it goes about what it does. From this perspective, intensive probation (IP) can be seen as simply another step in an inexorable movement away from the social work roots of probation work. IP, therefore, was a development which had keen support from some and equally strong opposition from others in the probation service. For some, IP was a logical step forward in the struggle to do something positive with serious offenders in the community, while for others it was yet another betrayal of traditional social work values.

HOME OFFICE RESEARCH STUDY No.133

This report presents the first phase of findings from a major study of IP carried out by the Home Office Research and Planning Unit. Chapter 2 sets out the origins of intensive probation and puts it into context; this chapter also discusses the methods used in the evaluation. Chapter 3 describes briefly the IP schemes which were included in the research and the kinds of offenders dealt with. Chapters 4, 5 and 6 contain case-studies of three IP schemes. And Chapter 7 pulls together the findings from the research and discusses their implications.

2 Background

The origins of intensive probation

The first point to emphasise in attempting to situate IP in its context is that the idea of intensive probation is by no means a new one. During the late 1950s a series of initiatives – which continued into the Sixties – took place in the USA whereby, essentially, probation caseloads were reduced with the intention that more of what was on offer would be delivered to offenders. In England and Wales the IMPACT (Intensive Matched Probation and After-Care Treatment) experiment took place in the first half of the Seventies, representing the culmination of research which had begun ten years earlier. This project had a considerable amount of resources devoted to it and was subject to detailed study by the then Home Office Research Unit, although both volumes of the report on the project scarcely total 75 pages (Folkard *et al*. 1974, 1976). IMPACT ended not with a bang but with a whimper. The second volume was published immediately after Stephen Brody's *The Effectiveness of Sentencing* (1976) and was perceived as contributing to the newly received wisdom that 'Nothing Works'. It is worthwhile adding, however, that the IMPACT studies have been the subject of recent reassessment which argues that they were unfairly perceived as demonstrating failure (see Roberts 1990).

Intensive probation, then, comes to us with a history; it carries a good deal of ideological baggage, not least an association with 'Nothing Works' and the perceived failure of probation to have any impact upon reoffending. But there is one key difference between intensive probation in its previous incarnation and the present initiatives. In the past intensive meant more social work, more counselling, more guidance; while today, intensive tends to mean a more rigorous and demanding approach to working with offenders. Though usually interpreted by its opponents as meaning no social work and all control, this is a crude and unfair caricature as many intensive probation schemes are still social work-based and remain rehabilitative at core.

The origins of IP are not simple and clear-cut; a variety of precipitating factors can be seen to lie behind the introduction of intensive probation, although it is difficult to order these in terms of their significance. Prison overcrowding was, of course, a key factor but it should be noted that the prison population of 17-20 year olds with sentences of up to 18 months (a key target group for IP schemes) began to decrease from 1985 onwards and had more than halved by 1990 (Home Office 1992a). To a certain extent IP was yet another in the long line of post-war policy initiatives which were devised to tackle prison overcrowding – attendance centres, community service, the suspended sentence, parole, day centres, probation hostels and bail information schemes.

Two closely related themes which lay behind IP were the need for effective punishment and the necessity of restoring judicial confidence in the work of the probation service. Prison was considered not to be particularly effective for many of those so sentenced – 'Imprisonment is not the most effective punishment for most crime' (Home Office 1988a) – but there was also a feeling that the existing community penalties were not as rigorous and demanding as they might be, especially if offenders were to be diverted from custody to these penalties. The Audit Commission report on the probation service emphasised this point by arguing that the increase in the use of the probation order and the community service order during the 1980s seemed to have been mainly at the expense of the fine and had been accompanied by increases in the use of custody (Audit Commission 1989). Linked with this was the idea that sentencers had lost the trust they had formerly had in the work of the probation service, and that it was vital that such trust should be restored (there was no real evidence that such trust had ever existed or that it had disappeared). One of the ways in which IP was expected to deliver effective punishment was another factor in its development – the need to reduce offending and thereby demonstrate that crime could be controlled.

The example of the considerable drop in juvenile involvement in the criminal justice system was also an important factor by showing that something could be done about what was commonly regarded as an intractable problem (between 1980 and 1990 the number of juveniles proceeded against in magistrates' courts fell from 139,000 to 54,000; see Home Office 1992b). Part of the reason for the drop in the number of juveniles being processed by the criminal justice agencies was demographic – the number of juveniles in the population was decreasing – and this would filter through to the 17-20 age group. But policies and practices which worked for juveniles would not necessarily work for young adults; the latter suffer from unemployment, homelessness, they may be married and have children, and they are more likely to be involved in the misuse of alcohol and/or drugs.

Costs also played a role in IP. Prison is a very expensive method of dealing with offending, and cheaper and equally – or possibly more – effective methods were desirable. Compared to other community penalties IP promised to be expensive – but less expensive than custody. Any cost advantage would be lost, however, if IP did not act to divert offenders from custody. And the example of the Medway Close Support Unit should be borne in mind; the cost per day was less than that at a detention centre, but the length of sentence at the Unit was twice as long as a detention centre order making the cost per order almost twice as high at the Unit (Ely, et al 1987).

The example of intensive probation in the USA was also a key background factor. Prison overcrowding, serious doubts about the efficacy of probation supervision (caseloads of several hundred were not uncommon), and a fiscal crisis whereby building more and more prisons was financially problematic were the driving factors behind the proliferation of American IP schemes. These can include a high number of contacts per week (either with the probation officer, a surveillance officer, a member of the offender's family or a sponsor) both face-to-face and by telephone, a period of community service, a curfew or period of house arrest (with electronic monitoring often used), employment/school attendance requirements, regular checks of police arrest records, random urinalysis, restitution, and payment of fees to offset the costs of supervision. Early reports on IP in the USA tended to be positive, stressing its effectiveness and advantages, but later studies have been more cautious pointing out failures to achieve full implementation and raising questions about the effectiveness of IP (for useful studies of IP in the USA see Byrne *et al*. 1992, Crime and Delinquency 1990, Federal Probation 1986, McCarthy 1987, Petersilia 1987, Petersilia and Turner 1991).

That such a variety of background factors should underlie IP is not unusual. Social policy in general is driven by many disparate factors and penal policy is no different in this respect. It should be noted, however, that IP may not be able to satisfy equally well all of the demands which may be made of it. Will it be able to reduce offending, reduce the prison population, provide effective punishment, keep sentencers satisfied, and reduce costs all at the same time? The expectations for intensive probation should not be pitched too highly, and it must be remembered that IP is very much a series of experimental initiatives. Indeed, the significance of IP may have changed since the time of its pre-implementation planning. With the hindsight available since the publication of the White Paper *Crime, Justice and Protecting the Public* (Home Office 1990a) and the introduction of the Criminal Justice Act 1991, IP can be seen as marking a transitional phase between those post-war policies aimed at reducing the prison population and the new emphasis on preventing and reducing crime.

The first ideas about more intensive forms of probation supervision can be discerned in the Green Paper *Punishment, Custody and the Community* (Home Office 1988a), but the first specific proposals appeared in a later discussion document *Tackling Offending: an action plan* (Home Office 1988b) which was circulated to probation areas in August 1988. This paper encouraged all probation areas to target young adult offenders and asked them to prepare and submit local action plans which would 'review their policies and practices relating to young adult offenders'. The paper went on to state that:

> Probation services in selected areas should set up "intensive probation" programmes exclusively for offenders who would otherwise receive custodial sentences. The courts should be involved closely in the design of the programme and the police should be kept in touch. The projects should be monitored, costed and evaluated. (emphasis in original)

Tackling Offending then went on to discuss various good practice guidelines for the proposed local action plans. Only towards the end of the paper was the theme of intensive probation taken up again:

> In selected areas, where there is a special need as shown by statistics of offending and/or rates of custodial sentencing of young adults, intensive probation (IP) projects could be set up. They would apply and test out a

5

> wide range of methods in a more concentrated fashion than would otherwise be possible. In particular, they should include use of methods which exercise a degree of control over offenders. Examples of these are 'tracking' schemes, and schemes in which the offender reports to the probation service at frequent intervals (and perhaps at unsocial hours) ....The Home Office will... discuss, initially with the probation service, the possibility of 'intensive probation' (IP) programmes being set up in selected areas.

IP was certainly not the focus of *Tackling Offending,* indeed, it was not much more than an afterthought. In the event, therefore, all areas began to prepare their local action plans as requested in *Tackling Offending*, with some being much further forward on developments along these lines than others (a full study of probation services' responses to the Tackling Offending initiative has been carried out by researchers at the University of Hull; see Bottomley *et al.* 1992). The IP proposals, having been judged to be of lower priority, were put on one side by Chief Probation Officers (CPOs). When Home Office plans for intensive probation were further advanced (six months later in February 1989), ten probation areas were approached. Despite the carrot of some extra resources, most of the ten areas were initially apprehensive. There was a feeling that having taken steps along the lines of developing action plans and discussing these with sentencers, it would be difficult to go back to sentencers and argue that there were further ideas which they would like to develop. There was, therefore, some considerable initial confusion about IP in so far as it was not differentiated clearly enough from the action plan suggestion, and, with the wisdom of hindsight, the approach to potential IP areas might have been better timed to take place at the same time as *Tackling Offending* was issued not 12 months or more later.

Intensive probation was intended to be an experimental, developmental initiative, and as a result there were few guidelines about how it should be put into practice and what it should look like. Apart from the understanding that IP was intended for high risk offenders who were likely to receive a prison sentence, there were certain expectations – as the first letter to the ten CPOs who were invited to set up IP schemes made clear:

> A range of methods might be used, but an IP programme must include the availability of a day centre requirement or a similarly demanding and intensive programme constructed under section 4A. All IP programmes should include arrangements for offenders to be either "tracked" or report frequently to probation officers.

Other elements which were seen as necessary for IP schemes included:

(a)   the setting up of rigorous referral and selection procedures in order that low risk offenders would not be subjected to IP and net-widening avoided;

(b)   a comprehensive and individualised programme which would be worked out with the offender and presented to the court;

(c)   a focus on confronting offending behaviour;

(d)   the use of a multi-agency approach whereby the skills of voluntary and statutory agencies would be utilised;

(e)   some evaluation of the schemes' success which would include the participation of ethnic minority and female offenders.

These rather general guidelines had advantages as well as drawbacks. A good deal of the detail of IP was being left to the initiative and imagination of individual probation services; there was scope for innovative projects to be designed by probation officers. In practice, however, very few services seemed to have the ability, space or time to grasp the opportunity offered them. Some services were already running or were planning to run schemes which were taken under the IP umbrella, while others were a considerable distance further back and starting from scratch.

A further problem was that all of the ten services approached were, to a greater or lesser extent, apprehensive of being seen to have failed in IP. The idea that areas were being encouraged to try out a relatively novel approach with few strings attached (and some extra resources involved) was viewed with some caution; there was a feeling that if IP was judged to have failed in an area then that area would be perceived as having failed in some way and Home Office disapproval would follow. As a result, IP initiatives were not as radical and innovative as might have been expected. Other factors also limited the ability to design new programmes quickly – local politics, bureaucratic procedures, and lack of imagination for example, at least in those areas which were starting from scratch with their IP schemes.

Of the ten areas which were approached by the Home Office, nine agreed to set up intensive probation schemes with a formal – and somewhat notional – start date of 1 April 1990; Berkshire, Durham, Gwent, Hampshire, the Inner London Probation Service, Greater Manchester, Northumbria, West Midlands and West Yorkshire. Three of these areas were already running schemes which were included under the IP rubric (Hampshire, Greater Manchester and West Yorkshire), and one (ILPS) failed to get a scheme off the ground during the two years of the project. The tenth area approached was not opposed to IP and considered that schemes in the county were very much along the lines of what the Home Office expected, but decided not to get involved with IP formally. This was partly for financial reasons, partly because of the amount of work which was being taken forward under the Action Plan initiative, and partly due to apprehension about the response of staff to what might be seen as a punitive approach to probation.

It was originally planned to set up a further ten IP schemes before the end of 1991 and Bedfordshire, Cheshire, Cumbria, Derbyshire, Devon, Essex, Leicestershire, Nottinghamshire, Northamptonshire and Staffordshire were invited to participate. For various reasons, only a few of these areas put IP schemes into practice.

Research methodology

Intensive probation was viewed from the start as an important development for the probation service, and it subsequently was seen as a possible forerunner for the proposal to set up a new combination order of probation and community service (provided for in the Criminal Justice Act 1991). IP pulled together several issues which the probation service had been grappling with for some time – amongst them the targeting of high-risk offenders, rigorous programmes of supervision, and the need to provide for ethnic minority and female offenders. It was, therefore, agreed that a detailed evaluation of IP would be necessary and the Research and Planning Unit was asked to carry this out.

As has been noted, however, IP was intended as an experimental initiative which was left in the hands of the probation services involved. As a result variations were not only to be expected in the forms which IP took, but were encouraged. A simple evaluation design concentrating solely upon a few outcome measures would have been inappropriate for such a project. The research design was built upon two aspects of evaluation: process evaluation and outcome evaluation (see Mair 1991).

All too often in research studies aimed at assessing the success or failure of an initiative we learn nothing of the initiative itself beyond perhaps a brief description of what it looked like at the planning stage. Anyone trying to interpret outcome measures in such a vacuum is severely handicapped. Outcome measures may suggest complete failure and a scheme is terminated; but if a study of the process of the scheme had been carried out it might have shown that the plans did not go into practice for various reasons (adequate funding was not available, potential participants in the scheme did not materialise), or that the scheme changed its nature when it was underway (committed staff left and replacements were unenthusiastic, a different target group from that intended was captured). In these circumstances a conclusion that the theory behind the scheme was a failure would be premature and unfair. It would also be unfair to condemn a scheme as a failure if it was intended as an experiment; the nature of experimentation is at least as likely to end in failure as success, and as much can be learned from the former as the latter.

A process evaluation will show how an initiative was devised in the first place and the reasons for this; it will show how it was put into practice and whether or not this differed from the blueprint; it will investigate developments over time and attempt to demonstrate why subsequent changes took place. By doing these things, a process evaluation provides the context within which outcome measures can be fully interpreted. To carry out this part of the study three IP schemes – those in Durham, Leeds and the West Midlands – were studied in detail to provide case-studies of the development and implementation of intensive probation. It is important to be clear on two points about these case-studies. First, they are not intended to be comparative; and second, they are not meant to be representative of IP. The reason for both of these caveats lies in the experimental nature of IP; as the design of IP programmes was left to probation areas the three areas are not comparable, and they cannot be seen as 'typical' of IP in any meaningful way. Durham was chosen because it was a small area and was setting up its scheme from scratch; West Yorkshire because it had two IP programmes which had been running for some time prior to the official start date; and the West Midlands because it was a large metropolitan area.

To complement the process evaluation an outcome evaluation has also been built into the research, but this will not concentrate solely on a simple analysis of reconviction rates as has been the case for many studies of penal sanctions. Reconviction rates are a problematic measure for assessing the success or failure of court sentences, and while they should certainly not be ignored their significance should be treated with some caution. For this research project, several outcome measures will be considered: reconviction rates (during the course of the IP programme as well as during subsequent normal supervision; and covering the time to reconviction, the offence for which offenders are reconvicted, and the sentence on reconviction), diversion from custody, financial costs, the views of sentencers, and the views of offenders. Because of the time-lag in examining reconvictions no analysis of recidivism will be included in this report; nor will there be any analysis of sentencing trends in IP areas for the same reason. A future publication will examine these aspects of IP. Where possible, it was intended to supplement these primary measures with a series of secondary measures which might be specific to IP programmes or the individualised schemes put together for offenders. These might include finding suitable accommodation or employment for offenders, help with tackling substance abuse or the use of leisure facilities.

Basic information on all those referred to IP programmes, recommended for IP in a social inquiry report, or sentenced to IP (for the sake of simplicity these three groups will be termed referrals) was collected from all participating areas for the duration of the project (1 April 1990 – 31 March 1992) at three times: at the time of sentence, at the conclusion of the period of IP, and at the conclusion of the period of normal supervision (data for this final period are still being returned). Seven areas supplied information for more than one year (depending upon the start date for their IP scheme), although Greater Manchester only ran their IP scheme for the first 12 months and supplied data for only 17 offenders.

A mail questionnaire was sent to all magistrates in the three case study areas, but it proved impossible to follow the same method for distributing the questionnaire in each area. In some Petty Sessional Divisions the clerk sent them to magistrates, in some the researchers could use a name but the questionnaire was passed on by the clerk, and in some the questionnaire was mailed direct by the researchers. A high response rate was not expected from the questionnaire and the method used did not help matters. As will be seen in the relevant chapters, the response rate varied according to the number of magistrates contacted. Durham magistrates were sent the questionnaire in September 1990; those in Leeds in November 1990; and those in the West Midlands in December 1990. One point which became clear was that receiving the questionnaire was itself a stimulus to some magistrates to find out about IP, although it is impossible to know just how often this occurred.

Researchers visited the three areas every few months (this is certainly not as often as is desirable, but represents the best that can be done with limited resources and competing demands) to observe the schemes and talk to all those involved about developments – probation officers and offenders especially.

The IP project is a major piece of work for the RPU and the approach adopted for the research is rather experimental. Dissatisfaction with earlier efforts to capture the complexities of measuring the effectiveness of sentences, and the need to take full account of the potentially innovative and developmental nature of intensive probation itself have contributed to the methods used.

3 Intensive probation in practice: an overview

This chapter provides a brief description of each IP project included in the research (including the three case studies which are studied in much greater detail in Chapters 4, 5 and 6), as well as those projects which were planned to make up the second group of ten schemes. Data from the monitoring exercise show the kinds of offenders who were being recommended for IP. From these descriptions of projects it should be possible to begin to assess how far IP schemes were innovative, whether there were key similarities between them, and the kinds of offenders they were dealing with. At the end of the fieldwork all IP areas were asked to send in a short report detailing the successes and failures as seen by those running the schemes, and where these were sent by areas they have been used.

Overall, a total of 1,677 offenders were referred for IP in the eight areas monitored. Almost all were male (95 per cent) and more than three-quarters were aged 25 or less. Problems were encountered with the collection of data on the ethnic origin of referrals, but at least six per cent were from ethnic minorities. 83 per cent of referrals were unemployed. The most common offence was burglary of a dwelling (26 per cent), with other forms of burglary (16 per cent), theft/handling (16 per cent) and violent offences (14 per cent) also common. Only six per cent were first offenders and 51 per cent had six or more previous court appearances leading to a guilty finding. 54 per cent had served a previous custodial sentence, and 42 per cent had spent at least some time on remand in custody in connection with their current offence. Almost two-thirds (64 per cent) were sentenced at the Crown Court. In all, 45 per cent of referrals were sentenced to IP; 37 per cent of those referred were sentenced to custody. As the following descriptions will show, these overall figures hide wide variations amongst the IP areas.

Durham

The North Durham Intensive Probation Partnership Project – or Gate Project – came into operation on 1 June 1990, initially available to two of the three PSDs in the North of the county, and was extended to the third a month later. The project was run as a partnership between Durham Probation Service (DPS) and a charitable company, Durham Training Enterprises (DTE). The setting up of the project was aided by a number of developments which were already under way prior to the Home Office initiative. There was already a considerable history of inter-agency co-operation between the local service and the voluntary sector. Moreover in this context, there had been specific discussion of setting up an alternative to custody project for young adults. Thus the seeds had already been sown prior to the publication of the Green Paper and *Tackling Offending*. This concurrence of events, combined with early, detailed and successful negotiations with the local branch of NAPO (The National Association of Probation Officers) were largely responsible for the scheme's almost universal acceptance amongst field teams.

The target group was broadly defined as offenders aged 17 to 25 at significant risk of custody – but there was a particular focus on burglars and offenders with a "complexity of needs" i.e. those with chaotic life styles and a number of social problems. IP orders were available at both magistrates' and Crown Courts and were made as probation orders with 4A requirements. The orders consisted of 60 'contact days', which were defined as days on which there was at least one face-to-face contact between project worker and offender.

The Gate Project was located in its own office, which was used mainly as an administrative base by the project manager (a main grade probation officer) and three project workers. IP in Durham differed from other probation orders in two main respects: first, a considerable amount of outreach work was carried out by project workers and second, orders included a number of components in addition to normal probation supervision. The outreach work often consisted of meeting offenders at their homes and driving them to day centres, offending behaviour groups or recreational activities. Frequency of contact during the early part of the order averaged four to five per week, but in individual cases could be as high as seven. Thereafter contacts decreased. Possible additional components on the order included an accommodation scheme, an employment scheme, offending behaviour groups and constructive use of leisure. Leisure activities could involve weight training, snooker, community work at a local hospital or environmental work. A number of offenders took part in these activities as part of the Duke of Edinburgh Award Scheme.

From June 1990 to March 1992 there were 95 attempted referrals to the project. In 16 of these cases a request for adjournment in order to assess suitability was rejected by the court. Of the remaining 79 offenders actually referred to the Gate, 58 offenders were accepted as being suitable for an IP order. Finally, of these accepted referrals, 45 (or 78 per cent) were given intensive probation orders by the courts. Information was also collected on a comparison group of 4A/4B referrals.

Nearly all the IP referrals were aged 17 to 25, whereas 35 per cent of the 4A/4B referrals were aged 26 and over. Only two of the IP referrals were female and all were white. Half of the IPP referrals and 44 per cent of the comparison referrals were convicted of burglary offences. IPP referrals had received their first conviction at an earlier age and a greater proportion (68 per cent) had previously received a custodial sentence than the comparison group. Despite the fact that the IPP referrals had a younger age profile, 68 per cent of them had six or more previous convictions, compared with 48 per cent of comparison cases. While 44 per cent of the IPP referrals were dealt with at the Crown Court, 38 per cent of the comparison group were so dealt with. All of the 13 offenders referred and accepted for IP but not given such an order by the courts were given custodial sentences.

Leeds

Two IP programmes were set up in Leeds, catering for two target age groups. The first, the Edge, was aimed at 17-20 year olds whereas the second, LISP, was aimed at young offenders aged 21 and over. Although both programmes intended to address offending and, at the same time, afford some public protection, they differed in many respects, e.g. the way in which they developed, the way in which they were managed and staffed and the structure and content of the programme. As with IP in Durham, the Edge was a partnership between the probation service and a voluntary body, the National Children's Home (NCH). It was funded by the Home Office and run by NCH workers and social work professionals from NCH premises. LISP, on the other hand, was entirely a probation programme, run by probation officers and probation service assistants.

The Edge was developed from scratch in response to the IP initiative whereas LISP had evolved from a previous programme for young adult offenders. LISP was greeted somewhat sceptically by main grade officers and NAPO who saw it as putting more emphasis on control than on helping the offender address problems. The Edge was not perceived as such a controlling programme, but it too was received with some mistrust since it was the first time probation officers in the area had been expected to delegate probation work to a voluntary organisation.

Both programmes targeted offenders at risk of custody in both the Crown and magistrates' courts. Referrals were made by the probation officer writing the social inquiry report and were considered by the IP managers and project workers (in the case of the Edge) to decide whether the referral was appropriate. There then followed an assessment period after which the referral would be accepted or rejected prior to sentencing.

At both the Edge and LISP, IP consisted of a 60 day probation order with a 4A requirement. The 60 days differed slightly in practice: the Edge saw offenders for a period of 60 days, i.e. two months, whereas LISP saw them 60 times, each contact counting as a 'day' whether it was for five minutes or an hour. The frequency of contact was initially high at LISP and became less frequent as the order progressed. At each project, an individualised programme was drawn up at the beginning of the order. This would identify problems to be addressed during contacts with programme or project workers, such as accommodation, unemployment, alcohol or drug problems. Neither the Edge nor LISP ran group work sessions. At LISP daily programmes were agreed with offenders in which movements and activities for the next day were planned. The programme worker could turn up at any time to check that the plan was in fact being carried out.

In total, 532 offenders were considered for referral for IP in Leeds – 233 at the Edge and 299 at LISP. Practically all referrals were male (97 per cent at the Edge and 96 per cent at LISP) and most were white (88 per cent at the Edge and 94 per cent at LISP). Ninety per cent of referrals to the Edge were within the target age range (17-20), as were 89 per cent of referrals to LISP (over 21). The majority of referrals to each project were considered to be at risk of custody: 79 per cent at the Edge and 88 per cent at LISP had Risk of Custody (ROC) scores above 70 per cent and around three quarters of referrals to each project were made via the Crown Court (71 and 75 per cent respectively). Eleven per cent at the

Edge were first offenders compared to three per cent at LISP; and one third had six or more previous convictions at the Edge compared to two thirds at LISP (these differences are probably a reflection of the different age groups targeted by each project). The most common offence for referrals at each project was burglary, either in a dwelling or other premises (51 per cent at the Edge, 41 per cent at LISP). Other offence categories for LISP referrals were theft/handling (19 per cent), violence (14 per cent) and drugs offences (12 per cent). At the Edge, other offence categories included robbery (11 per cent) and violence (11 per cent).

Of the 532 referrals, 200 (42 per cent) were sentenced to IP. Three quarters of these were sentenced by the Crown Court. A similar number (42 per cent of the total, 70 per cent of the remainder) received a custodial sentence.

Although both projects were acknowledged by probation management to be accurately targeting high risk young offenders, the feeling at the end of the two year monitoring period was that the service would continue to work with the voluntary body as long as it did not require probation service funding. As soon as funding dried up, the probation service would take over the programme for 17-20 year olds which would be run on the same basis as the programme for older offenders. In addition, this programme would provide a model for future implementations of IP in other divisions of the county.

West Midlands

The West Midlands IP initiative was focused on four large divisions in the West of the county. Service managers hoped that the introduction of IP could be used to implement common targeting criteria for high tariff probation orders and lead to more shared use of resources; thus the main aim of IP in the West Midlands was to encourage standardisation of practice across teams and divisions. Reflecting this agenda of standardisation, IP was to be delivered by all probation teams and there was therefore no IP office and no dedicated staff (save for administration).

It was intended that IP would replace existing 4A orders and become the sole high-tariff community penalty for the target age range of 17 to 21. The new order was to be marked by more intensive supervision and more use of multiple components. In effect this meant that, in addition to contact with the supervising officer being more frequent, the offender would be referred to one of two voluntary bodies which were working with offenders. One – the Rainer Foundation – aimed to help offenders find employment while the other – the ARK – focused on providing leisure facilities (mostly weight training). Although these components were considered useful to some offenders, they were not legally part of the order and so attendance could not be enforced.

The main difference for main grade officers between IP and probation orders with conditions was that, in order to recommend IP in a SIR, the officer had to fill out specially-designed, headed paperwork. This paperwork introduced a focused approach to recommending IP, including specification of the aims and frequency of probation supervision and providing for a contribution from voluntary bodies. However, this paperwork proved unpopular with main grade officers, who saw it as unnecessarily lengthy and cumbersome. Moreover, given that the voluntary contributions were not enforceable, most main grade officers saw the paperwork as a way of merely 'dressing up' an existing order to sell to the courts. There was also considerable scepticism expressed by field teams about working with employees from voluntary bodies, who they viewed as untrained for work with offenders.

IP started in the West Midlands in September 1990 and over a period of 19 months, 187 referrals for IP were made. The age of referrals ranged between 17 and 21 and six per cent were non-white; four per cent were female. Only 52 per cent of referrals had a risk of custody score of more than 70 per cent and fewer than half (47 per cent) appeared in the Crown Court. Thirteen per cent were first offenders and 29 per cent had more than five previous convictions. Thirty-eight per cent were charged with a burglary (either of a dwelling or other premises) and 18 per cent with violence. Eleven per cent were charged with theft/handling, and the same number with indictable motoring offences. Eighty-six offenders (46 per cent of referrals) were sentenced to IP and 58 (31 per cent of referrals) received a custodial sentence.

After 19 months, IP was officially wound up in the West Midlands. Senior management concluded that IP had successfully increased standardisation of practice: as a result of the initiative, there was widespread use of Risk of Custody scores in targeting SIR recommendations and a more general awareness of the potential for contribution from the voluntary sector. However, on the other hand, the implementation of IP had been marked by some confusion. Many main grade probation officers did not understand how IP was supposed to differ from other orders with requirements and were ignorant of – or confused by – changes in targeting criteria and practice guidelines. This led to considerable disaffection with local management and a cynicism with regard to the new order.

Berkshire

The Berkshire IP programme was based on an established day centre in Reading which, like most day centres, aimed to offer an alternative to an immediate custodial sentence (Mair 1988). IP in Berkshire began formally on 1 June 1990 with a target group of 17-20 year olds deemed to be at high risk of custody and who would be able and willing to co-operate with the programme. IP was available to both magistrates' courts and Crown Court, in contrast to the normal day centre order which was available only to the Crown Court. Offenders attended for 23 hours per week for 60 days if unemployed, and for 20 Saturdays if working.

IP involved several programmes in addition to the range of courses offered by the day centre (offending behaviour, group and individual counselling, sports, craft, etc.). A reparation scheme was compulsory with workshop projects aiming to help the elderly, disabled, play groups, and so on. A burglary programme aimed to confront burglars with the impact of their crimes, and involved the police and victim support schemes. While IP received a substantial number of referrals for offences of burglary, the number of orders made did not support a continuing, viable group with this focus and other common offences were included in this item of the programme (e.g. car crime). It was hoped to encourage offenders to take up six-month placements with Community Service Volunteers, but despite considerable efforts this did not succeed as offenders did not seem keen to move away from home and do voluntary work. During the period of research an adventure training week in Wales was run, and it was planned to develop this to take place three or four times a year. Individual action plans were prepared for offenders and it was emphasised that a follow-up programme would be arranged on completion of attendance at the day centre.

In total, 94 referrals were made for IP during the monitoring period, all of which were for offenders between the ages of 17 and 21. Six per cent of referrals were made in respect of females; 90 per cent of those for whom information was available (there were eight missing cases) were classified as white, and 78 per cent were unemployed. Forty two per cent had been convicted of burglary, 13 per cent of a violent offence, and 12 per cent of theft/handling. Only four were first offenders, and 35 per cent had six or more previous convictions; just over 30 per cent had had a previous custodial sentence. Sixty per cent were sentenced at the Crown Court, and 70 per cent of those referred were sentenced to IP; of the remaining 28 cases, most (21) received custodial sentences.

Gwent

The Gwent IP scheme was also based upon an existing day centre, and began operating on 1 September 1990 (limited resources and the need to modify buildings meant that the scheme could not start on 1 April). The target group was offenders at high risk of custody, with a focus on young adults and domestic burglars sentenced at the Crown Court. The usual programme ran for three days per week for 13 weeks with several days each month set aside for other optional activities (although one day each month was compulsorily spent on "community reparation"). For those offenders in work, education or training, an evening programme was run on two evenings each week.

IP led to more resources for the day centre and several extra staff were appointed, which led to some specialisation in the fields of employment, training, education and welfare advice. The core programme consisted of an offending behaviour group (one-to-one sessions also took place on specific offending issues), an alcohol education group and a social skills group. Highly individualised programmes of supervision were utilised mostly when an offender on the IP scheme had reoffended. In addition sport, drama, arts and crafts were included in the programme, and specialist groups were run whenever needs were identified, e.g. on HIV, drug misuse, sexism.

Although the Gwent scheme ran satisfactorily, its staff identified several problems. In the first place, the IP scheme was not seen across the probation area as a whole as a service-wide resource; it was isolated in a day centre in a specific location and many staff outside of the immediate area did not recognise IP as relevant to them. Attempts to change such views were largely unsuccessful. As a result, individual programmes of supervision for IP offenders which attempted to involve the offender's home area proved difficult to put into practice. Second, IP was well-resourced but seen to deal with few offenders and as having a relatively high breakdown rate. In contrast, the rest of the local service saw its workload increasing with no extra resources, and the consequence was that IP was not regarded in a positive light. There was a feeling that more detailed guidance about IP might have been helpful, although in the case of breach practice, for example, there was no easy answer. A rigidly enforced breach policy was needed, but if this was followed too slavishly then attendance would drop resulting in lower occupancy and less effective use of resources.

186 referrals were made to the Gwent IP scheme, with roughly one-third in the 17-20 age group, one-third aged 21-25, and one-third aged 26 and over. Only two offenders were female, and 85 per cent were unemployed. Forty two per cent of referrals were convicted of burglary, 17 per cent of violent offences and 15 per cent of theft/handling. There were no first offenders, and almost 70 per cent had six or more previous convictions; just over two-thirds had served a previous custodial sentence. Fifty five per cent were sentenced at Crown Court and of all those referred 42 per cent were sentenced to IP; the vast majority of those who did not get IP (103 cases) received custodial sentences (70 per cent).

Hampshire

The Hampshire IP schemes too were based on day centres in the county; two in the south at Portsmouth and Southampton, and one in the north at Basingstoke. All ran different programmes although they each targeted offenders who were at high risk of custody, particularly from the Crown Court. Each of the centres used other statutory and voluntary agencies in addition to probation staff, but the level of use differed from centre to centre.

The history of each of the three day centres influenced the way IP was implemented in each: the Southampton centre ran a rolling programme where successful referrals were fitted in whenever a space became available; in Portsmouth the programme was closed, which meant that offenders had to wait until a group had finished for a new group to begin the programme; the Basingstoke centre operated a modular programme where there was greater emphasis on designing individualised programmes. The length of each programme varied, and the kind of activities offered at each centre differed as did the amount of time devoted to them (for a full description of the three centres see Godson, Cureton and Swyer 1991).

The local service was aware of the inconsistencies which emerged from having three different systems in place, and efforts were being made to establish a common length for IP and to develop a core curriculum which would still permit centres to run programmes which were put together to address local problems. By working to increase consistency it was hoped that the confidence of sentencers in the programmes would be strengthened.

Intensive probation in Hampshire received 351 referrals, 40 per cent of which were for 17-20 year old offenders and 36 per cent for those aged between 21 and 25 (data were missing on age for 40 cases). Only eight referrals were made in respect of female offenders; three-quarters of those for whom information was available (there were 29 missing cases) were classified as white; and 88 per cent were unemployed. Forty seven per cent were convicted of burglary, 15 per cent of violent offences, and 17 per cent of theft/handling. In terms of their criminal history, five per cent had no previous convictions, and 63 per cent had six or more previous convictions; 62 per cent had served a previous custodial sentence. Eighty five per cent of referrals were sentenced at the Crown Court, and 47 per cent received intensive probation; of the remaining 186 most (88 per cent) were sentenced to custody.

Greater Manchester

The IP scheme in Greater Manchester was based on a 4A programme. It was first seen as a response to the Home Office 'Tackling Offending' initiative and, indeed, was begun as part of this initiative. Subsequently, the Home Office asked Greater Manchester Probation Service to consider the Young Adult Programme as an intensive probation programme and this was agreed to. Research has demonstrated the confusion which was felt by probation services in their response to the 'Tackling Offending' initiative (see Bottomley et al. 1992) and in this case the confusion between responses to that initiative and to the slightly later IP initiative is evident.

The scheme was based in Bury and targeted 17-20 year olds who were at risk of custody mainly in the Crown Court although the magistrates' court was not excluded. The programme ran on Tuesday and Thursday evenings for two hours each, and on Saturdays between 10.00 am and 4.00 pm for a period of 12 weeks; after this, participants continued to attend once a week for a further 24 weeks. The aim was to ensure that the programme would be convenient for employed offenders or those who might find work during the course of the order. Only two probation officers worked on the IP scheme which was focused around four components: offence avoidance, problem-solving skills, project work and group directed work.

The scheme was running before the start of the IP initiative – it began on 1 August 1989 – but it did not last for the two years expected and closed down in April 1991. This did not fit Home Office expectations for IP and suggests that there was some disagreement between the centre and probation services about what IP was meant to be. The Manchester rationale was that the programme was always intended as a temporary experiment to test the feasibility of IP. Problems had been encountered in identifying a target group of offenders, and it was considered that the scheme was no more effective – but more costly – than local conventional day centres. The two officers who ran the scheme experienced some difficulties in keeping it going as they were badly stretched in resource terms; and non-attendance led to increased costs and difficult decisions about when to breach.

Data were collected on 17 referrals, all of whom were aged between 17 and 21; two of those referred were female, and all but one were white. Three of those referred were employed. Seven offenders were convicted of burglary, five of violent offences and four of theft/handling. None were first offenders, and ten had more than five previous convictions; eleven had served a previous custodial sentence. Most (11) were sentenced in the magistrates' court, and ten of the 17 received IP; six of the remainder were sentenced to custody.

Northumbria

The Northumbria IP scheme (based in Newcastle) was a particularly interesting example of what could be done within the overall IP initiative, although it did not conform to the Home Office guidelines for IP. Once again, the scheme did not start from scratch but was based on work which was underway in response to the 'Tackling Offending' initiative and which was developed into an IP programme. The scheme began in April 1990 with a target group of 17-25 year old offenders, primarily those subject to probation orders although IP was also possible at the pre-court stage, on release from custody or even during a custodial sentence as part of a temporary release provision.

This interest in taking offenders who were not necessarily subject to a probation order was only one special characteristic of the Northumbria IP scheme. In addition, the scheme was voluntary and not tied to any special conditions added to a probation order, and it was modular offering a range of courses lasting for three or four days. The structure of IP was designed by field officers in an effort to avoid any marginalisation of the programme and to try to ensure that it was seen as relevant and useful to mainstream probation work. Each probation office in the Newcastle Division was represented on a steering group which helped in the continuing development of the project.

A wide range of courses and activities was on offer on the IP scheme. There were various group work courses run by the IP Unit staff and interested field officers; these included two general offending behaviour courses (one of which was for women only), a course on car crime, and a course focusing on aggression and violence. Other courses were offered in partnership with voluntary and statutory agencies which offered specialised help: a course on drug problems, on alcohol and offending, on assertiveness for women, and on employment and training opportunities. In conjunction with NACRO, the IP Unit also set up the 'Scope' project which ran music, drama, cookery, education and arts/crafts sessions. A motor project was also run by the IP Unit and NACRO. For women only there was a coping with stress course, and an animation workshop.

IP Unit staff were proud of their programme, and while it did not follow Home Office expectations of IP it did offer an innovative approach. The local service felt that the programme offered flexible, individualised packages which could be built up over time and permitted offenders to take advantage of them when they felt it was appropriate to do so. It was recognised that the courts would have preferred an order with conditions, but the success of the package seemed to provide proof that the courts could be won over if efforts were made. The Unit worked hard to target female offenders (as IP was expected to do) and was very successful in this respect; in the first year women made up 17 per cent of those attending IP courses, and in the second this figure increased to 23 per cent.

Finally, it is worth noting that while the Northumbria IP scheme was somewhat idiosyncratic in its approach, it may be that this way of doing IP stands a better chance of continuing after the introduction of the combination order than the other approaches discussed above. The other IP schemes described were based fairly closely on existing 4A or 4B requirements which might mean that in practice they could be difficult to differentiate from these requirements over time. With the advent of the combination order, as IP was not a statutory court order it could fade from the scene. With the Newcastle model, however, this would not be so likely and it is relatively easy to envisage IP fitting into the new requirements of the Criminal Justice Act; the new automatic conditional release system, for example, would seem to offer possibilities for the IP Unit.

During the two years of monitoring 215 people took part in the Northumbria IP scheme (unlike other IP schemes, data were collected on those participating in the scheme because of its voluntary nature); 37 per cent were under the age of 21 and 36 per cent were aged between 21 and 25. Nineteen per cent of those participating in IP were female, by far the largest proportion for any IP scheme monitored. Almost 80 per cent were unemployed. One-quarter of those who took part in IP had been convicted of burglary (because of the nature of the IP scheme, this may include some who had been so convicted and sentenced to, for example, probation and had subsequently agreed to attend an IP course; and some who had served a custodial sentence and agreed to attend an IP course after release from custody), one-quarter of theft/handling, and 15 per cent of a violent offence. Ten per cent were first offenders and 43 per cent had six or more previous convictions; 38 per cent had served a custodial sentence. Thirty nine per cent were sentenced (or had been sentenced) in the Crown Court, and IP was included in the sentence in one-third of cases; the remainder participated in IP as part of pre-court work, as part of a sentence they were already serving, or as part of post-custodial arrangements.

Other IP schemes

Some of the practical difficulties in translating policy into practice and in putting intensive probation schemes into operation can be shown by a brief discussion of the other IP schemes which were involved in the initiative.

The Inner London Probation Service was one of the original ten proposed IP projects, but theirs did not get off the ground during the two year period of the research. ILPS agreed to participate in the IP scheme but for reasons which remain unclear no progress was made. The plan was to base IP on 4B orders, but there were serious problems in recruiting staff from within ILPS to work on IP (there was some suspicion of an informal NAPO boycott of these posts). Funding was made to the voluntary sector to take part in the proposed IP programme, but there were no further developments.

South Yorkshire was also one of the original ten IP schemes, although it was not formally included in the IP initiative which started in April 1990. The local service had carried out a great deal of work in response to 'Tackling Offending' and had agreed procedures with sentencers and the local NAPO branch. South Yorkshire was willing to be part of the formal IP initiative but did not wish to be identified with the formal title of intensive probation. At the beginning of the initiative it was considered to be important that IP be seen as a coherent development and that all participating areas should refer to their schemes as IP. As South Yorkshire was not willing to jeopardise the work which they had done and risk confusing the courts, the service decided to withdraw from formal participation in the IP initiative. Representatives of the service continued to attend meetings about the initiative, however, and when definitions changed during the course of the experiments South Yorkshire was included again although it was too late to collect monitoring information by this time.

It was originally planned to introduce a second group of ten IP schemes in April 1991. The proposed second ten areas were Bedfordshire, Cheshire, Cumbria, Derbyshire, Devon, Essex, Leicestershire, Northamptonshire, Nottinghamshire, and Staffordshire, but IP schemes were not developed in all of these areas for several reasons. First, with the approaching introduction of the combination order and no firm clarification about how IP would fit into the new order there was a certain lack of interest in organising IP programmes (Nottinghamshire withdrew in order to concentrate its resources on implementing the Criminal Justice Act). Second, some areas had made their financial plans for the forthcoming year and unless extra funds were available the introduction of an IP programme was out of the question; the problem was exacerbated by the introduction of cash limits (this was the case for Bedfordshire, Cumbria and Northamptonshire).

The IP programme at Cheshire was similar to the Northumbria programme in that it was voluntary and based around a modular programme. The programme was, however, somewhat longer than in Northumbria and promised a minimum of 30 sessions drawn from a variety of modules. The scheme was limited to the Crown Court. In Devon, the IP programme was based on a 4A requirement, targeted on those aged 17-23 at high risk of custody and available to Crown and magistrates's courts. During its first year of operation (from 1 January 1991) the scheme did not attract as many referrals as expected (only 36) although a good deal of groundwork had been done with field teams and sentencers. This could simply be as a result of building up the scheme and numbers could increase in the second year. A total of 16 offenders were sentenced to IP in the first 12 months, seven in magistrates' courts and nine in the Crown Court.

The Derbyshire IP scheme began in October 1991. It was based on a 4B requirement, was only available to the Crown Court and limited to unemployed offenders (subject to review after some months of operation). Offenders attended one of two day centres for three days a week during 12 weeks. For two of these days offenders would be involved in group work concentrating on offending behaviour. alcohol misuse, social skills, anger management, etc. For the third day offenders would participate in the PACT scheme (a partnership between the local service, SOVA and APEX) which offered education, training and employment. In the first eight months of the scheme 32 referrals were made and eight IPP orders resulted.

The Essex IP programme was due to start in June 1992. Development had been delayed due to protracted negotiations with the local NAPO branch which had eventually passed a resolution against the scheme. The scheme was to be aimed at 17-25 year old offenders who were at risk of custody and appearing in the Crown Court, or at a magistrates' court for breach of a community supervision order. IP was to be based on a 4A requirement but also had a condition of residence at a probation hostel for a period of 17 days. During that time an intensive programme of work was planned (details of how participants in the IP programme would fit into the general regime of the hostel were to be worked out in practice).

IP in Leicestershire began in October 1991 and involved four new probation officer posts. These were created to work intensively with small numbers of targeted individuals – 17-25 year olds who were at risk of custody and had certain identified needs. IP was based on a straight probation order without conditions as there was a wish to differentiate it from the established 4A and 4B programmes in the county. Intensive, face-to-face work was to be carried out with offenders during the first three months of their probation orders, and IP was available to all courts in Leicestershire. During the first six months of the project 97 referrals were made which led to 52 recommendations for IP, 22 of which were successful. The framework for IP was expected to change with the introduction of the Criminal Justice Act; for example, IP could become a condition of a probation order.

Finally, the Staffordshire IP scheme was a partnership programme with National Children's Homes which offered courts a specified activities programme (4A) for 17-24 year old offenders at risk of custody. An evening group work programme catered for employed and unemployed offenders, while a daytime programme offered individualised packages for unemployed offenders. In the first four months of operation 57 referrals were made to the scheme; of these, IP was recommended in 37 cases and orders were made in 18 cases (six from the Crown Court).

Some conclusions

What can these brief descriptions of intensive probation programmes tell us about IP as a concept and how it was implemented? In the first place, although it may seem to be of little import, it is important to note that all areas did not begin IP at the same time as had been envisaged; some had been doing IP under another name, while some took months to organise a scheme and put it into operation. One consequence of different start dates is differential effectiveness even where other things are equal; any new initiative takes some time to settle down and find its feet, and one would expect to find a programme which had been running for some time to be more effective than one which had only been running for a few months. Delays in starting IP could be for various reasons, but they do suggest that probation services may not always be able to move quickly to develop innovations from the centre. Whether all probation services should be expected to be able to do this kind of thing is one issue; whether it is because the probation service as a whole prefers to move by consulting widely with its members which may slow change down is another. But the possibility of delay in implementing policy initiatives should be borne in mind.

INTENSIVE PROBATION IN PRACTICE: AN OVERVIEW

It is possible that related to such delays is the heavy emphasis of IP programmes on established 4A and 4B schemes. In their desire to set up IP programmes in line with Home Office wishes, it was no doubt easier for services to modify established schemes than to set up a new scheme from scratch. Associated with this is the confusion which was caused by the IP initiative following so closely on the heels of 'Tackling Offending'. All areas had moved to develop work following the circulation of this document and some had clearly gone too far to be able to respond to a further request to develop IP so soon after developing Action Plans. Indeed, the initial response of many of the first ten proposed IP areas was that they had made arrangements with local courts and it would be very difficult to return now and ask them to take on board IP. There was, therefore, a problem in differentiating IP from Action Plan work and several of the IP schemes were responses to the 'Tackling Offending' initiative.

The general guidelines set out by the Home Office for IP schemes were, for the most part, adhered to: efforts were made to target high-risk offenders and the data presented suggest that such efforts were successful, individualised programmes were worked out, other agencies were often used. But, as has been suggested these were usually tacked onto existing programmes. Innovative programmes were rare and did not tend to fall in with the notion that IP should be based on a condition added onto a probation order: in Newcastle IP was purely voluntary for almost anyone the local service came into contact with; in Leicestershire IP was carried out under the aegis of a straight probation order with intensive individualised work during the first three months; while in Essex it involved a 17 day residence at a probation hostel.

Finally, targeting varied from area to area. In a few cases, IP was available only at the Crown Court, while in others it was equally available to the magistrates' courts. The age-range differed from area to area. And there are obvious questions about consistency and uniformity when the length and intensity of IP varied amongst areas, and even at times within an area.

IP, then, was not a monolithic concept. But real innovation was uncommon, although it may be argued that this was never the aim of the initiative. This point will be taken up again in the concluding chapter. In the next three chapters, detailed case-studies of three IP areas are set out and many of the themes in this brief overview of IP schemes are discussed further.

4 The Durham IP Project

Origins

The setting up of an intensive probation project in Durham was aided by a number of developments which were already under way before the Home Office launched intensive probation (IP). There was already a long history of inter agency co-operation in Durham. In particular, Durham County Probation Service had worked with a charitable company, Durham Training Enterprise Limited (DTE)[1] and Durham County Social Services in developing an alternative to care and custody project for juvenile offenders. Named 'Challenge', this scheme was set up as a response to the circular on Intermediate Treatment sent to local authorities in 1983 (DHSS 1983). The partnership and the project proved successful and even at this early stage there was the intention of extending the initiative to young adults.

Although no firm developments took place over the next few years, the idea of enhanced probation for young adults continued to be considered at various times. In 1987 the Durham Probation Service Project Development Officer was involved with the Save the Children Fund (SCF) in developing an estate action project in Peterlee. In general discussions which accompanied this initiative, SCF expressed an interest in developing an alternative to custody project for young offenders. They had already set up a scheme of this kind in Scotland, which operated as a diversion from detention for 16 to 20 year-olds. A steering group was set up to co-ordinate the development of such a project, but eventually SCF decided they did not want to expand their work further in North East England, although they remained on the steering group. Quite separate from these developments, probation officers based in Consett had also indicated an interest in trying to set up a more intensive form of supervision for this age group. The combination of these influences resulted in DTE being approached and asked to take over the reins from the SCF, commissioning a feasibility study to look at the possibility of setting up a diversionary scheme for young adults.

The Steering Group concentrated on the north of County Durham, on account of the prevalence of young adult offending in Derwentside and Easington. This was thought to be associated with the closures of the steel industry in Consett and the mines throughout the Easington area. It was therefore the north of the county that was targeted for IP.

Thus, prior to 1988 and the appearance of the Green Paper, *Punishment, Custody and the Community* (Home Office 1988a), several possible models had already been mooted for co-operative working with voluntary agencies on an intensive supervision project for young adults. For various reasons (mainly to do with the non-availability of resources) little had been done about these proposals, but interest was rekindled with the publication

---

[1] The company was later renamed Durham Initiatives in Support in the Community (DISC), but will be referred to in this report as DTE.

of the Green Paper and *Tackling Offending* (Home Office 1988b). By the time the findings of the report commissioned by DTE were available, the management of Durham County Probation Service was taking an active interest in developing intensive probation in Durham.

Objectives

The Home Office requested areas to provide objectives, targets and performance indicators for proposed IP schemes. In the resulting document from Durham County Probation Service, *Project Objectives and Targets*, four chief objectives were identified:

1. To divert appropriate offenders in the age group 17-25 years from custodial sentences.

2. To demonstrate that the offenders can be safely supervised in the programme and that the reconviction rates at two years following sentence compare favourably to similar offenders who have served sentences of imprisonment.

3. To demonstrate positive impact upon the personal circumstances of offenders who are required to complete the IP programme.

4. To demonstrate that the approach can be cost-effective.

The first three of these objectives correlate closely with the three objectives outlined in a Home Office letter to CPOs of February 1989. Further information on the first of these objectives in *Project Objectives and Targets* described how successful diversion would be achieved through careful targeting, taking account of three factors: risk of custody, nature of offending and personal characteristics of offenders. With regard to risk of custody, offenders with a Cambridge Risk of Custody (CROC) score of 75 per cent or more were to be the main target group; a decision made on the basis of an analysis of SIR monitoring data collected in North Durham over the period August 1988 to July 1989. However, this analysis also showed that a 'significant minority' (in fact 40 per cent) of offenders receiving custody in the target age-group had CROC scores of less than 75 per cent. The fact that a considerable number of low risk offenders received custody during the monitoring period was thought to reflect the peculiar sentencing practice of two of the Petty Sessional Divisions in the catchment area. The importance of taking offence into account in the targeting of young adults at risk of custody was also brought out by the analysis of offence information from the SIR monitoring exercise. This identified burglary as an offence carrying a high risk of custody for the target age group. Nearly half of the 94 offenders aged 17-20 who received custodial sentences were convicted of burglary, as were over a third of the 99 imprisoned offenders aged 21-25.

With regard to the type of personal characteristics which should identify offenders as being suitable for IP, there was very little information in the written account provided to the Home Office or the guidance sent to sentencers and probation officers. Reference was made in the latter to targeting "those young adults for whom less intensive community-based options would not normally be considered by the Court, either by reason of the seriousness of the offence or the lack of motivation on the part of the offender." However, further information was derived from an early meeting with staff responsible for the development of the project, where the key to differentiating between offenders who were candidates for IP and other high-tariff offenders was noted to be "complexity of need". IP was to be aimed at offenders with chaotic life styles and multiple problems, such as lack of accommodation and employment, problems with DSS claims and substance abuse. This was to differentiate them from other offenders in this age group with high risk of custody, who might be eligible for community service or a day centre order.

In order to ensure that the offenders referred to the project reflected the target characteristics, 'gate keeping' procedures were to be carried out by Senior Probation Officers (SPOs) to ensure that main grade probation officers were applying the appropriate criteria in referring offenders to the project.

The second and third objectives require monitoring and research of reconviction rates and offender attitudes and these are addressed in the current study. The objective of cost-effectiveness is not explicitly mentioned in the Home Office letter to CPOs, but reference is made to schemes achieving a throughput of 50 offenders per year. Such numbers could not be expected of the proposed scheme in Durham, which was to cover the northern half of a comparatively underpopulated probation service area. A more realistic goal of 30 offenders per annum was suggested in the paper sent to the Home Office, once the scheme was fully operational.

Proposed nature and practice of the scheme

As the North Durham Intensive Probation Partnership Project – or Gate Project – was to operate only in the northern half of the county, it would draw on the petty sessional divisions (PSDs) of Durham, Chester-le-Street, Derwentside and Easington. Its target group was to be offenders aged 17 to 25 years, at significant risk of custody, and as a result it was hoped that a considerable number of referrals would be made from the Crown Court. The project manager was to be a probation officer, seconded from Durham County Probation Service but the provision for this officer was to be in addition to the normal probation staff complement for the Service. DTE was to provide two or three full-time project workers, clerical support and handle the administration and finance of the project. The scheme was based in two small rooms at DTE's Gilesgate office in Durham City.

The order was to be made in the form of a probation order with 4A requirements. 4A and 4B orders had been operating in County Durham before the inception of IP, and these orders would still be available for the target age group.

It was envisaged that the project manager would be responsible both to the Assistant Chief Probation Officer (ACPO) responsible for the project and the Chief Executive of

DTE. However, day-to-day management of the project manager was to be undertaken by the Chief Executive of DTE. The project manager would also be managed professionally by a Senior Probation Officer (SPO) in one of the probation teams covered by the scheme.

With regard to practice, offenders referred to the scheme were to be assessed for suitability through interview and by spending some time on the scheme itself, in a similar way to assessment at day centres in the county. If accepted, individual 'Plans of Action' were to be drawn up for each offender, drawing on a menu of different components. An action plan might consist of offence–focused counselling, group work, work on alcohol problems, literacy training, or help with employment and education. Some of these activities were to be included as conditions attached to the probation order under section 4A of the Criminal Justice Act 1982 and this part of the action plan was referred to as the 'primary contract'. Work undertaken in this category would include activities such as attendance at a group held in a day centre and a specified frequency of contact with their probation officer. Other components would be voluntary, such as help with accommodation and employment: the 'secondary contract'. Contact was to be intense in the early weeks of the order and project workers were to arrange 'outreach' meetings throughout the IP part of the order. Outreach work might involve meeting an offender and taking him/her to a group or checking that an agreed action was being carried out. However, throughout the order contact was also expected to be maintained with the offender's probation officer. In fact, the regular probation officer was to retain overall responsibility for the management of the order and was therefore to be responsible for any breach action.

The length of the order was up to 60 'contact days', analogous to the 60 days specified under a day centre order. However, unlike working days recorded for a day centre order, IP contact days were to consist of days on which there was any face-to-face meeting between project workers and offenders, however many and however short. Thus a contact day could, in theory, consist of a five minute meeting between project worker and offender or it could consist of two three hour contacts.

The plan of action was to be presented to the court as an agreed document, signed by the offender, the probation officer and the project manager. This document would be attached to a report, prepared by the project manager, assessing the defendant's suitability for the scheme. These documents would be presented as a supplement to the social inquiry report (SIR).

Implementation

Preparation

The scheme came into operation on 1 June 1990, becoming available to the Durham, Chester-le-Street and Derwentside PSDs to begin with and then becoming available to Easington PSD a month later. However, before this stage, quite extensive preparations had been made. A critical part of the successful planning and development of the scheme was the negotiations carried out with the local NAPO branch. The proposal for the scheme was discussed with them at a very early stage in the project's development and local support for the proposal was obtained at a meeting in December 1988. It was noted that the scheme met the national guidelines issued centrally by the union. Four points contained in the proposal were important in winning local agreement to the project:

1. That the manager was a probation officer appointed by the Probation Committee.

2. That any offender invited to enter the programme would sign the outline plan provided to the Court, indicating consent.

3. That the outreach workers would engage in helping (and social work activities alongside offenders), rather than purely monitoring their movements as a form of 'tracking'.

4. That the project would be run with new, rather than existing, resources.

The proposed scheme fulfiled these obligations, and thus the support of local NAPO representatives was assured, along with the support of many other probation officers who were sensitive to these issues. These early negotiations proved very important in the successful development and implementation of the scheme: the project would have been very hard to get off the ground without the support of the majority of field team probation officers.

It is interesting to note the reference to 'tracking' amongst the issues brought up by the local NAPO branch. This also proved to be a critical issue in the development of IP in the West Midlands (see Chapter 6) and the degree of acceptance of IP in West Yorkshire (see Chapter 5). There were obviously deep suspicions amongst many NAPO members that the proposed developments outlined in the Action Plan heralded the introduction of tracking schemes, similar to those pioneered in Leeds in the early 1980s, to the probation service as a whole. This is not altogether surprising if one considers that the Action Plan emphasised that IP projects "should include use of methods which exercise a degree of control over offenders. Examples of these are 'tracking' schemes...". 'Tracking' is an emotive word for many probation officers, who understand it in terms of control and punishment in the community, with the complete absence of social work input. It was unfortunate, perhaps, that the use of the term may well have induced a knee-jerk opposition to IP amongst many probation officers. As the development of IP in Durham has proved, a high rate of 'outreach' contact with offenders in the community can be perceived by offenders as less punitive than normal supervision in a probation office (see below). Having to visit a probation officer in an office in another town can be perceived as more intimidating and disciplinary than having less formal contact with a project worker in your own home.

Another important part of the preparation for the scheme was the introductory presentations made to magistrates' court liaison committees, clerks to the justices, judges and probation service field staff. Initial presentations were made two months prior to the start of the scheme's operation and these were followed up by subsequent meetings and presentations three months later.

Preparing the way for intensive probation in Durham was no doubt aided by the comparative receptiveness of the local probation culture. It was important that negotiations with the local NAPO branch were begun early on in the scheme's development. However, the receptiveness of the local union – and of field probation officers in general – to the idea of IP can also be attributed to Durham County Probation Service's considerable experience of working in partnership with the voluntary sector. Probation officers had already begun the cultural shift away from being the sole providers of support for offenders and IP fed in to this process.

Practice: work done on the order

For the most part, the types of activities included in IP orders were much as envisaged. 'Secondary contract' work such as seeking accommodation, employment or employment training was a common part of work on the order. The DTE housing scheme, Durham Access Resource Team (DART), was used to find homeless offenders accommodation, or in other cases, to help offenders move out from their family homes to their own flat. Help with employment proved more difficult to deliver. Early on in the scheme's history, DTE was able to fulfil its potential in providing either Youth Training or Employment Training for offenders on IP. However, in early 1991 there were considerable cuts in the number of places available on Employment and Youth Training for unskilled workers. This seemed to be due to a decrease in funding for training courses which had small numbers reaching a certain grade of National Vocational Qualification (NVQ). A large number of agencies either stopped providing training for unskilled workers or went out of business. As a result, training schemes for offenders, who are mostly unskilled, disappeared both within DTE and elsewhere in County Durham. This posed major problems for the Gate scheme, working as it did with unskilled offenders in an area of the country with a very high level of unemployment. However, in September 1991 DTE (by now renamed DISC) set up a new offender employment project, using further funding from the Home Office. While not targeted specifically at offenders on IP, this scheme has been used by the Gate project and a number of IP clients have obtained training and employment.

An important feature of the Gate project is the emphasis put on constructive use of leisure time. While this had always been an objective of the scheme, the lack of employment training facilities over much of 1991 seems to have increased the emphasis put on this type of activity. Weight training was taught by one of the project workers, and a volunteer taught offenders how to play snooker at a local club. In order to add more purpose to these activities, a number of offenders chose to take part in the Duke of Edinburgh Award scheme (DEAS), which is available for people under 21 years. Although each time an offender went to the sports centre and met the project worker, this meeting constituted a contact, much of the work done on the DEAS was voluntary. Weight training and snooker counted as only one of the components of the DEAS – the 'skills' component. Participants also had to involve themselves in a number of other activities, such as community work and a camping expedition. As part of his DEAS, one offender was working with mentally handicapped patients at a local hospital under the supervision of a local magistrate who did voluntary work in the hospital.

A further development in DEAS activities came later in the study period, through an association with the Groundwork Trust. This charity offered placements for offenders on IP to work on environmental improvement projects in the countryside. Offenders were taken on as assistants, responsible for supervising groups of volunteers, including the physically or mentally handicapped. Work done included clearing up colliery sites and planting trees along footpaths. In one particular case, an offender was travelling two hours by public transport in order to work on the project and later obtained a placement on a conservation course.

The leisure pursuits were obviously popular with many offenders, but some scepticism was expressed amongst field teams as to the benefit of this type of work. In particular, snooker was seen simply as a means of keeping offenders off the streets, with little chance of any lasting benefit. The point was made that few of the offenders could afford to practice their snooker skills once they completed their orders, due to the entrance fees charged at most snooker clubs. However, given the dearth of employment opportunities in the Durham area and the patchy provision of employment training, it could be argued that the DEAS work was one of the few options available. It should also be emphasised that much of the work done on the Duke of Edinburgh Award Scheme was very demanding, and required considerable self-motivation on the part of the participant. Another benefit of some of the physical activities was that in some cases it seemed to lead to close relationships being struck up between offenders and project workers. However, ultimately it was up to the individual offender whether or not he/she got involved with the DEAS – some grasped the opportunity which could lead to considerable achievements, others chose not to.

The other main type of work done on the scheme was attendance at groups. Offenders attended day centre groups on offending behaviour, employment, social skills, literacy and driver re-education. Midway through the study period, the project manager was instrumental in setting up a burglary group and an autocrime group. These schemes were run by the Durham County Probation Service group work co-ordinator and were available to the whole of North Durham, but were set up in response to the needs of the IP. As a general policy, project workers accompanied offenders on their first attendance at a group, by way of support and introduction. They might accompany him/her a second or third time but would then leave the offender to attend on his/her own. Although there was no actual contact between project worker and offender, once the offender was going to the group alone such attendance did count towards the order's 60 day contacts.

Apart from the activities described above, there was also a considerable amount of outreach work of a more general nature. IP participants were often helped in sorting out financial difficulties with the DSS, or with accommodation problems. It was made clear that if there were any personal problems, IP participants could ring the office and a project worker would visit them if possible. One offender interviewed after the IP part of his order, described being helped in the relationship difficulties he had been having with his girlfriend. Another offender was visited because she reported feeling depressed and ill. This type of work seemed to be greatly appreciated by offenders on IP – but as one of the project workers pointed out, there was a tendency for the project workers to feel like a free taxi service.

Structure of the order

Frequency of contact with project workers was intended to be intensive in the first few weeks and then gradually decrease towards the end of the order. Contacts during the early part of the order averaged four to five per week, but in some cases the figure could be as high as seven. Thereafter, depending on the needs and progress of the individual, the rate of contact was decreased. Both project staff and field team probation officers were aware that the cross-over from IP to normal probation supervision represented a dangerous time for offenders. After a period of intensive supervision on the IP component, offenders were only to be seen once a week by their probation officer. The IP team was aware of this problem, and efforts were made to 'wean' participants off the intensive component before they went on to normal probation supervision. However, field staff expressed the view that this rarely happened. To an extent, project workers were reactive: if offenders were in difficulties, they usually responded. It was therefore difficult to cut down the number of contacts where offenders were particularly dependent on their project workers. On the other side of the cross-over period, field teams were aware of the problem and made special efforts to see offenders more frequently during the early stages of the remainder of the probation order. But it was difficult for them to replace the kind of intensive supervision and support the IP participants were used to. Project workers impressed upon participants that they could still contact them after they had left the IP project, but such contact could only be rare, given that the project was encouraging offenders to cope independently with their lives.

An issue that arose quite early in the scheme's development was the extent of normal supervision that offenders should receive from their probation officers during the intensive phase of their IP order. In theory, offenders on IP were supposed to receive normal supervision from their probation officers, meeting them at least once per week. However, the project manager found that in some cases supervision of IP cases was rather perfunctory. This was borne out by interviews with officers in the field teams who reported a tendency to see IP clients less, in the knowledge that they were receiving adequate support from the project workers. An attempt was therefore made early on in the project to stress the importance of partnership between project workers and probation officers. Nevertheless some officers interviewed towards the end of the study period still referred to giving IP clients low priority, especially when they had high caseloads.

Management

During the first half of the study period, the management structure for the project seemed to be somewhat confused and over-complicated. While the project manager was a main grade probation officer, she managed three members of staff and held considerable responsibility for the scheme. There was therefore considerable need for backup from more senior colleagues. While it had originally been envisaged that day-to-day management of the project manager would be the responsibility of the chief executive of DTE, this arrangement did not seem to come to fruition. During the early stages of the scheme the project manager was managed in the main by her ACPO in the probation service. However, during the autumn of 1991 the ACPO post was vacated and the new ACPO adopted a more remote management style, allowing more input from DTE. The SPO responsible for the project manager's professional management gave up his role after six months due to other work commitments and was replaced by another SPO in the Derwentside area. Then towards the end of the study period, this SPO moved to another area of the county and, at the time of writing, there was no permanent replacement. Most of the time the project manager was therefore responsible to a SPO, an ACPO and the chief executive of DTE. Having three different managers had obviously proved quite complicated, especially early on in the scheme's development. There was some evidence that the project manager was unsure which manager to turn to for advice on particular issues. However later changes in staff seemed to have led to a clearer allocation of managerial responsibility.

Partnership

There were a variety of views expressed about the partnership between DTE and Durham County Probation Service. Those directly involved in the scheme seemed to find the partnership a complementary one. DTE could provide the financial and administrative resources, and the probation service was left to the professional issues. Indeed there was a considerable advantage to having DTE in charge of the finances: they were capable of reacting to the needs of the scheme without going though the bureaucratic processes of the local probation service. DTE obtained an office for the scheme, printed fliers, and found the finances for extra secretarial resources rapidly in response to the scheme's needs. On the negative side, early on DTE did not prove to be the force needed to provide youth and employment training and was unable to have much of an input on the professional side. Because of this, the view was expressed in some field teams that DTE were not pulling their weight, and that the probation service would have been better off without them. However, this would seem to be due primarily to the low visibility of the type of work that DTE contributed – as well as a degree of innate hostility on the part of some probation officers to the involvement of voluntary agencies in supervising offenders.

Certain probation staff seemed to be ambivalent in the degree to which they welcomed the idea of partnership. During early phases of the project there were indications that the responsible ACPO was somewhat wary of the involvement of DTE and seemed reluctant to hand over half of the management of the project to DTE. For his part, the chief executive of DTE felt that the work should either be seconded or not – rather than left somewhere in the middle. This situation changed with the arrival of the second ACPO, who seemed happy to allow DTE to take on most of the management responsibility for the scheme.

Another frustration cited by the chief executive of DTE concerned the involvement of DTE in offence-based work. The local NAPO branch had included as one of their criteria for supporting the Gate project, an undertaking that DTE would not be involved in offence counselling: a task they felt should be left to qualified probation officers. The parts of IP which were farmed-out to DTE were essentially support services – accommodation and employment projects. The chief executive of DTE felt that to draw the line here was arbitrary, and restricted the extent to which voluntary agencies could get involved with multi-agency initiatives with the service. He pointed out that project workers were inevitably involved in offence counselling in any case. This view was reinforced by interviews with project workers, whose work included asking offenders about their current behaviour, trying to ensure that they were not reverting to criminal activities. Indeed, in actuality, it would be very difficult to distinguish between offence counselling and providing other types of support – often offenders' criminal behaviour is part of a cycle of drinking, drugs, or 'mixing with the wrong people'. Thus, the issue seemed to be conveniently fudged: while DTE officially steered clear of developing group provision centred on offending behaviour, project workers on the ground were frequently involved in offence counselling.

Practice: findings from the monitoring data

Referrals and targeting

From June 1990 to March 1992 there were 95 attempted referrals to the project. In 16 of these cases a request for adjournment in order to assess suitability was rejected by the court. Of the remaining 79 offenders actually referred to the Gate, 58 offenders were accepted as being suitable for an IP order. Finally, of these accepted referrals, 45 offenders were given intensive probation orders by the courts. While an objective of the scheme had been to take on 30 orders per year when fully operational, it was thought unlikely that this would be achieved in the first year. This was borne out by the monitoring data: in the first twelve months 20 orders were made: over the next 10 month period there were 25.

As well as collecting data on IP referrals, information was also collected on a comparison group of day centre referrals. This group consisted mostly of offenders referred for 4B orders, but also included some 4A referrals who were to attend a group at a day centre as a 4A condition. In the following subsections, referrals to the Gate are compared with the comparison group of 4A/4B referrals.

Type of court

There were two main paths of referral. First, offenders could be referred to the Gate for assessment while the court was adjourned for a SIR and then, if accepted, an IP recommendation could be presented to the court without the need for any further adjournment. Alternatively, a recommendation for referral to the IP project could be made in a SIR. In this case, if the court accepted the proposal, a further adjournment would normally need to be made to allow the scheme to assess the suitability of the offender. While a large proportion of cases referred from magistrates' courts followed the first path and were referred while the SIR was being prepared, virtually all the Crown Court cases followed the second path and were referred during a second adjournment. As a result, the majority of cases where the court declined to adjourn for assessment were from the Crown Court (12 out of 16).

Referrals from magistrates' courts constituted the majority of the early referrals to the scheme, but Crown Court referrals picked up after the first few months and at the end of the study period constituted 44 per cent of all referrals made to the Gate (32 out of 72 where information was available). While many of the early reports were prepared at short notice, courts were increasingly prepared to adjourn cases in order that offenders might be assessed for suitability for an IP order.

The comparison group of 4A/4B referrals was slightly less likely to be Crown Court cases, with 38 per cent (50 out of the 129 cases where information was available) coming from the Crown Court.

Age

The target group of the Gate project was 17 to 25 year olds.

Table 4.1
Age groups of IP and 4A/4B referrals

| Age in years | Referrals | | | |
| | IP | | 4A/4B | |
	n	%	n	%
17 to 20	37	(48)	46	(35)
21 to 25	38	(49)	44	(33)
26 to 30	2	(3)	28	(21)
31 and over	-	-	15	(11)
Total[1]	77	(100)	133	(100)

[1] Information was unavailable for two IP referrals.

As might be expected, the large majority of the IP referrals fell inside the 17 to 25 year age groups. Only two older offenders were referred. The rest of the referrals were divided equally between the 17 to 20 and 21 to 25 age group. By comparison, a considerable proportion of the 4A/4B referrals were in the older age groups.

Gender, ethnicity and employment status

With regard to gender and ethnicity, only two of the 79 IP referrals were female, one of whom was rejected and all the referrals were white. A similar picture was true of the comparison group, although a slightly higher proportion of women were referred (seven out of 133). Very few of the referrals were in work, six per cent of IP and comparison referrals alike being employed at the time of referral.

Offence

In order to function as an alternative to custody, the Gate project would have to target offenders who had committed serious offences and were likely to receive custodial sentences. The monitoring form therefore requested information on the most serious offence committed by offenders.

Table 4.2
Offences committed by IP and comparison group referrals

Offence		Referrals		
	IP		4A/4B	
	n	%	n	%
Violence	7	(9)	12	(9)
Burglary in dwelling	17	(22)	51	(38)
Burglary in non-dwelling	22	(28)	8	(6)
Theft/Handling	11	(14)	19	(14)
TWOC/TADA	7	(9)	10	(8)
Criminal damage	7	(9)	6	(5)
Indictable motoring	4	(5)	16	(12)
Other	4	(5)	11	(8)
Total	79	(100)	133	(100)

Large proportions of both IP and comparison referrals were convicted of burglary offences. Interestingly, the comparison group was convicted of a larger proportion of burglaries in a dwelling – 38 per cent compared to 22 per cent of IP referrals - but a much smaller proportion of burglaries in a non-dwelling. Including both types of burglary, half the IP referrals had committed burglary offences, compared with 44 per cent of the comparison group. It would therefore appear that the scheme had successfully targeted burglars, who were defined as a group particularly likely to receive custodial sentences in the paper *Project Objectives and Targets*, although many of these will have been in the less serious category of burglars of non-dwellings.

The two groups received referrals from similar proportions of other offender groups, although indictable motoring offences were more common in the comparison group and criminal damage more common in the IP group.

Data were also collected on the number of other offences that offenders were convicted of when referred to the IP or day centres, excluding offences taken into consideration. There was a considerable difference between IP and comparison group referrals. While 18 per cent of IP referrals were convicted only of the single, principal offence, this proportion was 38 per cent for 4A/4B referrals. Seventeen per cent of IP referrals were convicted of between six and ten additional offences, compared with seven per cent of the comparison cases. Offenders referred to the Gate therefore seemed to have committed large numbers of offences, which would seem to suggest that they were at considerable risk of custody.

Criminal history and risk of custody

Various measures were included in the monitoring to measure tariff position or risk of custody. The reliability of some of these measures is hard to ascertain: it became clear in the course of interviews with probation staff that the availability of accurate information on previous criminal history seemed to vary considerably. It is probable that in some cases information was drawn from sources such as probation records, rather than police or CPS records – or even from the offender. However, this information was gathered by field probation staff and then relayed to clerical officers filling out the monitoring forms, and so the quality of the data should be comparable for the IP and comparison groups.

In some of the following analyses it should be borne in mind that the age ranges of the IP and comparison group referrals are quite different. This is likely to affect some of the measures of criminal history, in that younger offenders have had less time to pick up convictions.

In her research on the Crown Court, Hedderman (1991) has found that the remand status of a defendant can have a strong and independent effect on the decision whether or not to impose a custodial decision. Whether or not a defendant was remanded in custody was therefore included in the monitoring as an indicator of tariff position.

Table 4.3
Remand status of IP and 4A/4B referrals

| Remand status | Referrals | | | |
| | IP | | 4A/4B | |
	n	%	n	%
On bail	32	(43)	96	(76)
In custody	14	(19)	22	(17)
On bail then in custody	7	(9)	8	(6)
In custody then on bail	21	(28)	-	-
Total[1]	74	(100)	126	(100)

[1] Information was unavailable for 5 IP referrals and 7 4A/4B referrals.

From Table 4.3 it is clear that a considerably smaller proportion of the IP referrals were bailed throughout the remand period: while 43 per cent of the IP cases were bailed throughout, the corresponding proportion of 4A/4B cases bailed throughout was 76 per cent. Similar proportions of both groups were remanded in custody throughout the remand period, and similar proportions of both groups were first given bail and then remanded in custody. However, while 28 per cent of IP referrals were first remanded in custody and then given bail, none of the 4A/4B cases were so treated. This probably represents the courts bailing defendants who had already been remanded in custody in order to allow assessment for suitability for an IP order. However, it is unclear why this practice was not followed for 4A/4B referrals.

Age at first conviction was requested to give an indication of the starting point of offenders' criminal careers.

Table 4.4
Age at first conviction

Age at first conviction in years	Referrals			
	IP		4A/4B	
	n	%	n	%
Under 14	24	(39)	16	(12)
14 to 16	27	(44)	50	(38)
17 to 20	9	(15)	49	(37)
21 and over	2	(3)	17	(13)
Total[1]	62	(100)	132	(100)

[1] Information was unavailable for 17 IP referrals and 1 4A/4B referral.

Table 4.4 shows that over a third (39 per cent) of IP referrals received their first conviction when they were under 14 years of age, compared with 12 per cent of comparisons. A much larger proportion of the comparison referrals were aged 17 and over at their first conviction. It should be noted that there are a large number of missing cases for the IP group, but this cannot account for the differences outlined above. With regard to referrals who had no previous convictions, there was only one such referral to the IP scheme and eight to day centres.

Information was also collected on the most serious previous offence and the most serious previous disposal. Previous offence information was broadly similar for the two groups, although more of the IP referrals had been convicted of a violence offence (22 per cent compared with 11 per cent of 4A/4Bs). Previous disposal data were also broadly comparable: 68 per cent of IP referrals had previously received a custodial sentence, compared with 63 per cent of comparison referrals. However, it is with this type of measure that the difference in age range between the two groups becomes significant. Intensive probation referrals, being younger, are less likely to have committed so many previous offences, and may therefore be less likely to have received a custodial sentence.

The most simple criminal history variable is the number of previous convictions. Again the difference in age range between the IP and comparison referrals will mean that the IP group have had less chance to accumulate previous convictions.

Table 4.5
Number of previous convictions

| Number of previous convictions | Referrals | | | |
| | IP | | 4A/4B | |
	n	%	n	%
None	1	(2)	8	(6)
1 to 5	20	(31)	61	(46)
6 to 10	24	(38)	43	(32)
11 to 15	17	(27)	14	(11)
Over 15	2	(3)	6	(5)
Total[1]	64	(100)	132	(100)

[1] Information was unavailable for 15 IP referrals and 1 4A/4B referral.

Table 4.5 shows that despite their younger age profile, the IP referrals generally appeared to have more previous convictions than the comparison group. The average number of previous convictions was eight for the IP referrals and six for the 4A/4B referrals. There were considerably more offenders referred to the Gate project with between 11 and 15 previous convictions. While 27 per cent of the IP referrals fell into this category, only 11 per cent of the comparison group had this number of previous convictions.

Perhaps the most sensitive measurement of tariff position collected through the monitoring exercise was the risk of custody (ROC) score. Durham Probation used version II of the Cambridgeshire Risk of Custody Scale, which draws on various measures of risk, such as gravity of offence, sex and criminal history to produce a percentage likelihood of a custodial sentence. Quite marked differences were found between IP and 4A/4B referrals.

ROC scores show that both IP and comparison referrals were high tariff, with over half the referred offenders receiving ROC scores of over 70 per cent. However, proportionately more of the IP cases were in the highest category, with 44 per cent scoring 100 per cent, compared with 20 per cent of 4A/4B referrals. Very few IP referrals had ROC scores of less than 50 per cent. If one considers the age discrepancy between the two groups, these results become all the more significant. The Cambridgeshire ROC scale only takes account of whether an offender is a juvenile or an adult – there are no other age criteria (Bale 1989). As older offenders are more likely to score highly on the criminal history variables included in the score, this biases the comparison group towards receiving higher ROC scores.

Table 4.6
Risk of custody scores

Risk of custody	Referrals			
(percentage)	IP		4A/4B	
	n	%	n	%
0 to 50	4	(6)	24	(19)
51 to 70	19	(27)	28	(22)
71 to 99	17	(24)	49	(39)
100	31	(44)	25	(20)
Total[1]	71	(100)	126	(100)

[1] Information was unavailable for 8 IP referrals and 7 4A/4B referrals.

The fact that the offenders referred to IP were at serious risk of receiving a custodial sentence was borne out by interviews with probation officers and offenders in the field. Invariably, probation officers described IP referrals as very high-tariff, and many proffered the opinion that certain offenders would definitely have received a custodial sentence if they had not been placed on the Gate project. Indeed, the view was expressed that some of the offenders were too difficult to supervise, and very likely to reoffend: as one officer put it, "She [the project manager] has done herself no favours". As will be discussed in a later section, offenders on IP who were interviewed also expressed the opinion that they would have received a prison sentence had they not received an IP order.

Variations in referral rate

Throughout the study period, there was considerable variation in the referral rate between individual probation offices. One probation office in particular referred only two offenders to the scheme. Officers at this office seemed to find it more convenient to use the local day centre, which was located in the same district. However, the only other team with a local day centre in the same town had the highest referral rate of all the teams. An alternative explanation could lie in the SIR practice followed by the 'low referral' team. It was usual for high tariff SIRs to be prepared by day centre staff, who presumably were more likely to refer clients to their own centre than to the IP.

Mention was also made, during interviews with SPOs, of variation between individual officers. It was suggested that some officers were wedded to a traditional casework approach to supervising offenders, and therefore found it difficult to hand on responsibility for various components of an order to a project worker. Other officers were more open to new ways of working with offenders, or actually welcomed the opportunity to off-load on to others what they considered to be some of the more tedious work on an order.

Other targeting criteria

While the monitoring data show that the project seemed to be successful in targeting young high-tariff offenders, there were other features which were intended to identify the ideal candidate for IP. IP referrals were to be distinguished from other high-tariff offenders by their chaotic lifestyles and their multiple social problems. While information on social problems was not recorded on the research monitoring forms, some data was available from SIR monitoring forms filled out for internal purposes. This form was filled out by field team probation officers and recorded "offending related factors". These consisted of a range of problems including alcohol, drugs, accommodation, family difficulties and lack of social skills. Unfortunately, SIR forms were not received for the whole sample of referrals – only 36 were received of the 79 IP referrals and 104 were received of the 133 comparison referrals. Nevertheless, there is no reason to believe that the forms obtained are in any way unrepresentative. The average number of problems listed for the IP cases was 2.4 and the average for the comparison group was 1.8. While this would seem to indicate greater "complexity of need", it should be noted that some of the problems listed are likely to be age-related. IP referrals were much more likely to be recorded as having problems of "peer group influence" and "boredom/need for excitement". These differences could be explained in terms of the difference in the age-range between IP and 4A/4B referrals. On other problems the two groups were broadly similar, although there were a higher proportion of IP referrals with substance abuse problems. Cases referred to IP did therefore seem to have multiple problems, but this may be hard to disentangle from the fact that people in this age group tend to have a considerable number of social problems in any case.

The issue of the targeting of IP was also addressed through interviews with field teams. For the most part, field teams seemed to have a firm grasp of the IP target group. Most officers were aware that IP was supposed to be high tariff and targeted at disorganised offenders with multiple social problems, although the relative emphasis placed on these criteria often varied. A common response was that IP and day centres occupied a similar position on the sentencing scale, but that IP cases were too chaotic to fulfil a day centre requirement. However, one officer referred to IP cases being at the very top of the community disposal tariff, with a very high risk of custody and a high risk of reoffending.

A final factor that was linked to the targeting of IP was the motivation of the offender. In early guidance sent to magistrates and probation officers, explicit mention was made of targeting "those young adults for whom less intensive community-based options would not normally be considered by the Court, either by reason of the seriousness of the offence or the lack of motivation on the part of the offender." However, the failure of a number of offenders on IP early on in the scheme's development led to some disillusionment amongst IP staff and a reconsideration of this aspect of targeting practice. It was decided instead to target offenders with motivation to change. If offenders were to draw up lists of 'secondary contract' activities that they were to undertake voluntarily, this would require self-motivation in any case.

From referral to sentence

As mentioned above, of the 79 offenders referred to the project, 58 were accepted as being suitable for an IP order. At least one reason for rejection was obtained in 17 of these 21 cases. In seven cases, at least one of the reasons for rejection was that the offender failed to keep appointments. In four cases there were further charges for new offences or breach of bail conditions – in one case the referred offender was charged with murder. Three offenders did not want to join the project, three moved address, two needed psychiatric treatment and in one case the single reason given was that there was no scope for social work intervention. It proved hard to follow up these cases to sentence, but in the 13 cases where this was achieved, nine received custody.

In the majority of cases the probation officer making the referral was the same officer responsible for the order once it was made, but this did not always happen. Staff moves sometimes meant that officers had to take on orders referred by others.

SIR recommendations for IP were made in 57 of the remaining 58 referrals. In the other case, no explicit SIR recommendation was made but a Gate assessment report was presented to the court, which put forward the case for an IP order. Of the 58 accepted referrals, 45 offenders actually received IP orders from the courts. All of the 13 offenders who were accepted by the Gate but did not receive an IP order were given custodial sentences. This is an important indication that the accepted IP cases were at considerable risk of custody. By comparison, of the 117 4A/4B referrals that actually received SIR recommendations for a 4A/4B order, just less than half (57) actually received such a sentence. Of the other 60 offenders, 44 received custodial sentences and the remaining 16 received suspended sentences, community service, probation or fines.

Offenders given an IP order did not differ in any significant way from the total group referred to the scheme, although there was a tendency for them to be slightly lower tariff. This seemed to be associated with different rates of acceptance of recommendations for IP between the Crown Court and magistrates' courts. Of the 58 offenders accepted by the scheme, 32 were magistrates' court referrals and 26 were Crown Court referrals. While magistrates courts made IP orders in 30 of the 32 cases recommended for IP, the Crown Court made only 15 orders out of the 26 recommendations. As Crown Court cases were more likely to have a high risk of custody and be charged with more serious offences, this led to a slightly less serious group of offenders actually receiving orders. A similar process occurred with the comparison group of 117 cases that received SIR recommendations for 4A/4B orders: 56 per cent of the magistrates' court referrals received such an order, compared with 36 per cent at the Crown Court. The Crown Court cases had committed more serious offences and had higher risk of custody scores. This therefore led to slightly less serious offenders receiving orders.

A comparison of offenders sentenced to IP, 4A/4B and prison

The following analyses are based on three groups: the group of 45 offenders who actually received IP orders; the 82 offenders known to have received custody (22 of the IP referrals, 44 of the 4A/4B referrals and all the 16 cases where adjournment was refused); and 63 cases that received 4A/4B orders (the 57 orders referred to in the last section plus six orders made without a SIR recommendation).

Offence

There were some interesting differences amongst the three groups in the principal offence.

Although numbers in the offence categories are often quite small and are therefore susceptible to variations due to chance, there do seem to be differences amongst the groups. Perhaps most notable are the proportions of cases falling into the two burglary categories. Offenders given 4A/4B orders had most commonly been convicted of a burglary in a dwelling – with a third so convicted. An even greater proportion of the custody group had been convicted of this offence – 45 per cent. A much lower proportion in both of these groups had been convicted of a burglary in a non-dwelling. This situation is reversed for offenders given IP, with a third convicted of a non-dwelling burglary offence and half this proportion being convicted of a dwelling burglary. Taken with the evidence presented earlier on referrals, this does suggest that the Gate Project has targeted and "won" the less-serious burglars, although there were no indications from the interview material that this was a conscious objective.

Other differences amongst the three groups include the higher proportion of violent and car-related crime amongst the 4A/4B group, and the low proportion of offenders convicted of theft/handling and criminal damage amongst the custodial group. But the low number of cases makes drawing firm conclusions impossible.

Table 4.7
Offences committed by the three sentence groups

Offence	Sentence					
	IP		4A/4B		Custody	
	n	%	n	%	n	%
Violence	3	(7)	7	(11)	5	(6)
Burglary in dwelling	7	(16)	21	(33)	37	(45)
Burglary in non-dwelling	15	(33)	6	(10)	10	(12)
Theft/Handling	7	(16)	10	(16)	8	(10)
TWOC/TADA	4	(9)	4	(6)	7	(9)
Criminal damage	4	(9)	5	(8)	1	(1)
Indictable motoring	2	(4)	7	(11)	5	(6)
Other	3	(7)	3	(5)	9	(11)
Total	45	(100)	63	(100)	82	(100)

Comparisons were also made amongst the three sentence groups on the number of other offences with which they were charged. Only a fifth of the IP group were charged with no other offences, compared with over a quarter of the imprisoned group and nearly half of the 4A/4B group. The average number of extra offences for the IP and custody groups was three, and the average number for the 4A/4B group was 1.3.

Age

The age ranges of the IP and 4A/4B sentence groups were very similar to those of their referral groups (see Table 4.1). The custody group showed a similar profile to the 4A/4B group, except for a slightly lower proportion of offenders aged 26 and over. The average age for the three groups was 20 for IP, 23 for custody and 24 for 4A/4B.

Criminal history and risk of custody

As has been discussed with reference to the referral groups, it should be remembered that the age differences amongst the sentence groups may militate against the IP group scoring highly on various measures of criminal history. The three sentence groups differed in terms of the proportion remanded in custody.

Table 4.8
Remand status of the three sentence groups

Remand status	Sentence					
	IP		4A/4B		Custody	
	n	%	n	%	n	%
On bail	19	(42)	46	(79)	34	(43)
In custody	7	(16)	10	(17)	29	(37)
On bail then in custody	5	(11)	2	(3)	9	(11)
In custody then on bail	14	(31)	–	–	7	(9)
Total[1]	45	(100)	58	(100)	79	(100)

[1] Information was unavailable for five offenders given 4A/4B orders and three imprisoned offenders.

As can be seen from Table 4.8, IP cases resemble those given imprisonment in terms of the proportion given bail from the start. Forty-two per cent of IP cases and 43 per cent of offenders sentenced to imprisonment were not remanded in custody at all, compared with 79 per cent of 4A/B cases. However, while most of the remaining custody cases received remands in custody, most of the remaining IP cases were initially remanded in custody and then given bail. So, as with those referred to IP in Table 4.3, nearly half (47 per cent) of the offenders given IP were initially remanded in custody, two-thirds of these cases were later given bail, presumably in order to allow them to be assessed for suitability for an IP order. Therefore, the important point to notice from Table 4.8 is that very similar proportions of offenders given IP orders and prison sentences were initially remanded in custody – around half of each group, but less than a fifth of the offenders given 4A/4B orders were so remanded.

Quite large differences were also found amongst the three sentence outcomes on age at first conviction. While an examination of the most serious previous offence found few differences between the three groups, most serious previous sentence proved more interesting.

Table 4.9
Age at first conviction for the three sentence groups

Age at first conviction in years		Sentence				
		IP		4A/4B		Custody
	n	%	n	%	n	%
Under 14	16	(38)	5	(8)	16	(23)
14 to 16	21	(20)	28	(43)	23	(32)
17 to 20	4	(10)	20	(30)	28	(39)
21 and over	1	(2)	12	(18)	4	(6)
Total[1]	42	(100)	65	(100)	71	(100)

[1] Information was unavailable for three offenders given IP orders and eleven imprisoned offenders.

Table 4.9 shows that over a third of offenders given an IP order were convicted of their first offence while still under 14 years of age. By comparison, 23 per cent of imprisoned offenders and eight per cent of offenders given 4A/4B orders were convicted at this age. Much larger proportions of these sentence groups were first convicted in the 17 to 20 year age group. Very few offenders given custody or an IP order were first convicted over 21, but 18 per cent of 4A/4B offenders fell into this category. Thus, from this analysis, the offenders given IP seemed to have started their criminal careers earliest, with offenders given 4A/4B orders starting their criminal careers considerably later and imprisoned offenders fell in between the two. However, it should be noted that by definition, IP offenders could not be convicted for the first time over the age of 25 – so age again obfuscates the picture.

Table 4.10

Most serious previous sentence for the three sentence groups

Most serious previous sentence	Sentence					
	IP		4A/4B		Custody	
	n	%	n	%	n	%
Custody	28	(64)	31	(52)	61	(78)
Probation (+/- requirements)	9	(20)	12	(20)	8	(10)
Community service	7	(16)	8	(13)	4	(5)
Other	–	–	9	(15)	5	(6)
Total[1]	44	(100)	60	(100)	78	(100)

[1] Information was unavailable for one offender given IP, one given a 4A/4B order and four imprisoned offenders.

The proportion who had previously received a custodial sentence varied between the three sentence groups. Seventy-eight per cent of the offenders sentenced to imprisonment had previously received a custodial sentence. This compared with 64 per cent of the IP group and 52 per cent of the 4A/4B group. Thus, offenders sentenced to IP seemed to be midway between the other two groups on this measure of criminal history.

Turning next to previous convictions, offenders given IP orders seem to have more previous convictions than either of the other groups.

Table 4.11

Number of previous convictions for the three sentence groups

Number of previous convictions	Sentence					
	IP		4A/4B		Custody	
	n	%	n	%	n	%
None	–	–	2	(3)	–	–
1 to 5	9	(21)	35	(56)	32	(45)
6 to 10	19	(44)	17	(27)	25	(35)
11 to 15	13	(30)	7	(11)	11	(15)
Over 15	2	(5)	2	(3)	3	(4)
Total[1]	43	(100)	63	(100)	71	(100)

[1] Information was unavailable for two offenders given IP and eleven offenders given 4A/4Bs.

Compared to those who received custody or a 4A/4B order, there was a considerably smaller proportion of offenders given IP orders with less than six previous convictions. While well over a half of the offenders given 4A/4B orders and 45 per cent of imprisoned offenders had received less than six previous convictions, just over a fifth of the IP group were in this category. There was a higher proportion of IP offenders than other sentence groups in each of the ascending previous conviction categories. The average number of previous convictions bears out this picture: the IP group had an average of nine previous convictions, compared with seven for the custody group and six for the 4A/4B group.

Finally, the sentence groups were compared on risk of custody scores.

Table 4.12
Risk of custody scores

| Risk of custody | | Sentence | | | | |
| (percentage) | IP | | 4A/4B | | Custody | |
	n	%	n	%	n	%
0 to 50	2	(5)	16	(27)	4	(5)
55 to 70	13	(30)	15	(25)	13	(17)
71 to 99	13	(30)	22	(37)	20	(27)
100	16	(36)	7	(12)	38	(51)
Total[1]	44	(100)	60	(100)	75	(100)

[1] Information was unavailable for one offender given IP, three given 4A/4Bs and seven given custodial sentences.

Table 4.12 shows quite clearly that in terms of risk of custody, the Durham IP group lies between the custody and 4A/4B groups. Only two of the IP cases had ROC scores between 0 and 50. A similar proportion of imprisoned offenders had ROC scores of this level, but over a quarter of the 4A/4B cases had ROC scores between 0 and 50. The sentence category with the greatest proportion in the 55 to 70 category was the IP cases, and interestingly, 4A/4B cases had the greatest proportional representation in the 71 to 95 category. However, it is the 100 per cent ROC score group where the greatest disparities between the sentence groups are evident. While over half of the offenders sentenced to custody were given the highest possible ROC score, over a third of the IP group were so scored and only 12 per cent of the 4A/4B group were so scored.

Average ROC scores show that offenders on IP seem to be closer to the custodial group than to the comparison group: the average percentage risk of custody for IP orders was 83, compared with 87 for the imprisoned group and 67 for 4A/4B orders.

Conclusions

The Durham IP seems to have been successful in targeting defendants at serious risk of custody. There are two notes of caution that should be sounded: first, there is some evidence that while burglars have been successfully targeted, these are the less serious, non-residential burglars. Second, there is an indication that some of the most serious defendants targeted for IP at the Crown Court were not won. Nevertheless, those offenders actually given IP orders were clearly higher tariff and at greater risk of custody than the comparison group of offenders given 4A/4B orders. Making allowance for the younger age group of the IP cases, it seems that they are closer to the custodial group than the comparison group in terms of criminal history and risk of custody.

Views of sentencers and offenders

Magistrates' attitudes

For the four petty sessional divisions (PSDs) covered by the Durham IP scheme a total of 191 questionnaires were sent out; 146 responses were received (a response rate of 76 per cent), and of these, 96 (66 per cent) stated that they had heard of the local IP scheme (in one of the PSDs a majority claimed that they had not heard of the project). Table 4.13 sets out what respondents understood the aims of the IP scheme to be.

Table 4.13
Aims of the Durham IP project

Aim	Number of mentions
Alternative to/reduce the use of custody	68
Reduce offending	29
More intensive supervision	24
Treatment geared to the needs of the individual	9
Provide an effective community disposal for serious offenders	7
Provide individual and group supervision	4
Rehabilitate offenders	4
Provide another community sentence	3
Other (incl. tackling offending behaviour, cut costs, improve social skills)	6

By far the most popular response about the aims of the project was that it was intended to divert offenders from imprisonment and thus reduce prison overcrowding; that the project should seek to reduce offending and offer more intensive levels of supervision were also common responses.

Table 4.14 lists what the magistrates considered offenders would do during their attendance at an IP scheme.

Table 4.14

What offenders might do on an IP scheme

Activity	Number of mentions
Tackle individual problems	36
Examine offending behaviour	34
Group work	22
Learn social/vocational/leisure skills	18
Comply with requirements	17
Community work	10
Receive guidance/training/rehabilitation	9
Develop discipline/control	7
Keep in regular contact with probation officers	4
More demanding than normal supervision	4
Other (incl. practical activities, group therapy, constructive hard work, learn respect)	14

It is interesting to note that despite the Home Office emphasis on greater control of offenders, the responses of magistrates indicate quite strongly that they saw intensive probation as involving mainly social work tasks; responses covering more control and discipline are much less common than those covering more welfare-oriented activities. Whether this is a result of the way in which the Durham IP scheme had been 'sold' to magistrates is not clear, but it would seem that this is a possibility.

Tables 4.15 and 4.16 list the kinds of offences for which magistrates thought they would use IP and the kinds of offenders they might place on the project.

Table 4.15

Offences for which IP might be used

Offence	Number of mentions
Burglary	34
Car	31
Public order	23
Theft	22
Drug/alcohol related	21
Alternative to custody	18
Motoring	10
Criminal damage	8
Recurrent offences	7
Violence	5
Other (incl. non-violent offences, sex offences, imprisonable offences, fine default)	25

Table 4.16

Offenders who might be placed on IP

Offender	Number of mentions
Persistent offenders	36
17 to 25 year olds	25
Those at risk of custody	22
Those who can be helped	23
Those who have failed on probation/CSO	11
Those with alcohol/drug problems	4
Serious offenders	2
First offenders	2
Other (incl. the homeless, unemployed, those with a chaotic life-style)	7

There is an interesting range of offenders and offences seen as appropriate for intensive probation; on the one hand burglary is precisely the kind of offence which IP is expected to tackle, while motoring and public order offences may not be serious enough. There may be a question mark raised about the emphasis on persistent offenders as suitable for IP; the new Criminal Justice Act 1991 hopes to change the culture whereby offenders are sentenced as much for their criminal record as for their current offence, but this culture appears to be heavily embedded in the use of IP.

Not surprisingly, given that the programme had only been running for a few months, of the 96 respondents who had heard of the Durham IP scheme, only 11 (11 per cent) had visited it.

Magistrates were asked how they saw IP fitting into the range of sentencing options which were available to them and Table 4.17 sets out their responses. It seems from the table that there are rather different and vague views about the place of IP.

Table 4.17
"How do you see IP fitting into the range of sentencing options available?"

Position	Number of mentions
Another option	22
Alternative to custody	21
Last chance before custody	12
More intensive form of supervision	8
Between probation and custody	4
Alternative to a community service order	4
"Well"	4
Other (incl. too soon to say, depends on the offender, where hope of rehabilitation)	6

Finally, respondents were asked about the advantages and disadvantages of IP and Tables 4.18 and 4.19 set out responses.

Table 4.18
Advantages of IP

Advantages	Number of mentions
Reduce offending	21
Focus on the individual	16
Diversion from/reduce the use of custody	14
Help offenders to realise there are other options to offending	12
More intensive supervision	11
More help with problems	11
Gives serious offenders the chance to change	8
Rehabilitation in the community	7
Instil self-respect/discipline	4
Last chance for offenders	3
Saves money	3
Other (incl. alcohol/drug counselling, agreed contract between officer and offender, various agencies involved, none)	12

Table 4.19
Disadvantages of IP

Disadvantages	Number of mentions
Offenders may see it as a soft option	39
Public may see it as a soft option	8
Magistrates may misuse it	7
Under-resourced	6
Not intensive enough	5
Risk of further offending as community-based	4
Labour intensive	4
None	4
Too much commitment required by some offenders	3
Insufficient suitable staff	3
Group contamination	3
Other (incl. male-oriented, narrow age range, available for too few, might be too late, normal probation neglected)	13

Overall, there were fewer disadvantages mentioned than advantages. The latter seem to display a tension between the more controlling aspects of IP and its more helping aspects, between the 'tough' and the 'tender'. With regard to the former, clear possible drawbacks are identified, but the major problem for magistrates is that offenders may perceive IP as a 'let-off'.

Other comments on IP were on the whole optimistic in tone, wishing the scheme well but pointing to the need for highly skilled officers with sufficient resources to ensure that IP worked.

Judges' attitudes

One judge was interviewed about the Durham IP scheme and, in the event, his comments applied at least as much to the Newcastle scheme. He was in favour of IP generally, and was happy with the information he had seen about the schemes. IP was seen as an alternative to a custodial sentence and particularly appropriate for burglars. Its advantages were that it might make offenders stop and think, and should therefore lead to reduced offending. On the whole, it was a little too soon to make any final judgements about IP and time would tell.

Offender interviews

Eleven semi-structured interviews were carried out with offenders towards the end of the intensive phase of their IP orders. Three interviews were conducted at the Gate office, two at field probation offices, four at a youth club and two at offenders' homes. All interviews were conducted with only interviewer and interviewee present, and all interviewees were male, there being few females on intensive probation and none in the final stages of their IP orders when the interviews were conducted.

Early reactions to being on IP

Without exception, the offenders were relieved to have been given a probation order. All thought they were at risk of custody – and most expressed the view that if they had not been put on IP, they would definitely have received a custodial sentence. Estimates of the prison sentences they faced varied from nine months to two years. However although relieved not to have been imprisoned, two offenders reported feeling a certain degree of ambivalence. One offender said that he was not so happy to get a probation order "with strings attached": although he had thought custody the most likely sentence, he had assumed the alternative would be a "straight" probation order. Another offender thought he might have received a CSO as an alternative to custody, although he had already been on CS once before.

There were mixed reactions to the first two weeks on the order. As has been described, contacts were especially frequent in the first phase of the order. While most offenders seemed to appreciate the attention, others found it rather difficult at first. At one end of the scale, an offender described IP as "magic" from the start and another described how early on, IP had got him doing things and stopped him being bored and lonely. At the other end, one respondent had found the first couple of weeks difficult: he had not trusted his project worker at first, and had been wary of having a complete stranger come round to his house so frequently. However, while some offenders were initially wary about strangers appearing on their doorstep, none of the offenders found this a lasting problem.

Content of the order

Nearly all the offenders interviewed attended at least one group course during their IP order. The most frequently attended was the burglary group, which catered largely for IP offenders. Of the six respondents who attended the group, four described the course as worthwhile. Two of these referred specifically to how the course had increased their awareness of the impact their offending had on the victim. Of two offenders who found the course a waste of time, one described going over the same ground again and again and the other said that each time he had said anything, he had been contradicted or told to "shut up".

Five offenders mentioned attending a drinking and offending group at Peterlee Day Centre. Only two expressed positive opinions. One young offender related how he had never connected his drinking with his offending behaviour before attending the group. Once he had tackled his drinking problem, things had got a lot better and he had stayed out of trouble. Of the three offenders who were critical of the course, one offender expressed the view that sitting around talking about drinking problems did no good. As soon as the group was over he went straight down to the pub and got drunk. Another expressed the view that it was boring and that "they just took the mickey out of you".

Finally, three offenders attended one of two motor offence groups. One offender attended the autocrime group, run by the group work co-ordinator. He had found the group useful, but what he really needed was the money to take the Driving test. Two respondents had attended a driver re-education course at Peterlee Day Centre – one had found the course useful, the other said it had taught him nothing.

A number of the offenders received help with accommodation or employment, often through DTE. Council flats were found for three offenders, and this help was welcomed. One offender described how DTE had helped him get a two-bedroomed flat in a better area of town, "away from the roughs". Providing help with employment was more problematic. Much of the area of County Durham covered by the Gate project is economically very depressed, with unusually high rates of unemployment. There was therefore considerable scepticism expressed by offenders and probation officers alike about the possibility of finding employment. Moreover, as has been described, there were cuts in Employment Training funding for unskilled workers over the study period. Nevertheless, a number of offenders interviewed received help they considered to have been worthwhile. The ASTEP (Advice and Support, Training and Employment) scheme run by DTE, had aided offenders in preparing CVs and applying for jobs, and three offenders were either working or training for employment through the Gate. On the other hand, others had found ASTEP a waste of time, or had applied for employment training and found that no placements were available.

The other main component of IP in Durham was constructive use of leisure. All the offenders interviewed partook in at least one activity as part of their IP orders, save one who was ill and receiving sickness benefit. The most common activity was snooker, but a number also did weight training, badminton, camping or conservation work. Only one offender was negative about this aspect of the Gate. He felt that leisure pursuits would not keep people out of trouble and that the project should focus more on offending behaviour and how to stop it. However, for the most part offenders enjoyed participating in these activities. The view was often expressed that if it were not for the Gate they would not have had the opportunity to pick up these new skills or interests. Two respondents thought that boredom had been a major cause of their offending in the past, and that constructive use of leisure time would prevent them reoffending in the future.

While most of these activities were potentially skills that could contribute to the DEAS, only five of the offenders interviewed actually set their sights on an award. One motivation for undertaking what seemed to be a quite challenging course was that the certificate would carry some weight with employers. Many of the respondents had few or no qualifications and the DEAS was seen as a way of gaining an award which would look good on a CV.

In conclusion, opinions were divided on most components of the IP order. However, it is interesting to note that all the offenders were positive about at least one part of their order: it was not the case that individual offenders were responsible for all the negative views expressed. The leisure activities were popular with the large majority of offenders interviewed. It should be noted that the single respondent who was critical of this side of IP was at the top of the age range for the project. It could therefore be that this type of supervised, physical activity is more suitable for younger offenders. The least popular components of the order seemed to be the groups. Perhaps this is unsurprising, they are not presumably designed exclusively for the enjoyment of offenders.

Comparison of IP with straight probation

From the offenders' perspective, the chief difference between normal probation and intensive probation seemed to lie in the type of relationship they had with their project worker. With one exception, respondents were full of praise for their allotted project worker. Those allotted a male project worker tended to describe their relationship in terms of friendship: to quote one offender "I've got on with X like a good mate – as if I'd known him for years". Male project workers were variously described as "a good mate", "a great bloke" and "a good laugh". However, some respondents also referred to being able to talk to their project workers about their problems and getting good advice from them. The female (senior) project worker was described as someone they could talk to, and someone who helped them with personal problems. One offender described how he had confided in her about his drug problems, which he had told no-one else about.

These positive comments about the IP workers were made in response to the question of how project workers differed from probation officers. By comparison, probation officers were often described as less accessible: "more like schoolteachers", telling them what to do, and breaching them if they did not do it. Project workers were seen as friends, in whom respondents felt they could confide, and who were able to provide help if they were in need – they were able to come out at short notice in an emergency. Nevertheless, three of the respondents mentioned having good relationships with their probation officers – and one of these found contact with his probation officer considerably more useful: "I could learn more from one session with a probation officer than the whole of the IP order with my project worker". But it should be stressed that this was the only offender who was critical of his project worker.

A number of factors seem to be associated with the differences between probation officers and project workers identified in the interviews. First, and most obvious, project workers are essentially out-reach workers. This proved very popular with most offenders – they did not have to make a journey into town for a supervision session. Also, they felt more at ease in their own environment – visits to probation offices were described as intimidating and often involved hanging around. Furthermore, the fact that the IP workers were mobile, out-reach workers meant that they could react to emergencies – several offenders described getting into difficult situations and being "rescued" by their project worker. While probation officers may often do the same, they are inevitably more desk-bound and less reactive. A second factor is the fact that the project staff were not trained probation officers. Nearly all the respondents were aware of this fact. Relationships seemed to be less formal as a result – perhaps partly because the decision whether or not to breach offenders lay not with the project worker but the responsible probation officer. A third factor is the nature of much of the work done on IP. Being engaged in physical activities with project workers did seem to break down potential barriers. This was particularly obvious when observing a weight training session, where project worker and offender took it in turns to work out on a particular machine in the gym. The project worker described how this proved to be a relaxed situation to discuss any issues that might be troubling an offender. Finally, a significant issue is the age of the offender. Project workers seemed to be 'parent figures' for many of the offenders (and this could have serious disadvantages in terms of dependency when finishing the intensive phase of the order). However, there appeared to be a tendency for older offenders to be more cynical about forming such attachments. It is perhaps significant that the respondent who was critical of his project worker was one of the oldest of the group interviewed.

Overall assessment and suggestions for improvement

The large majority of offenders interviewed were positive about their overall experience of intensive probation. Most described being considerably better off having completed the IP phase of the order, compared with their position when they had been sentenced. Many described being less likely to offend, or more likely to get employment, or simply glad not to be in prison. However, in one or two cases, while the overall assessment of IP was positive, there were some qualifications. One offender described how ultimately it was up to oneself whether one reoffended or not, and as he had already made up his mind not to get into trouble again, IP was a bit of a waste of time. Another offender admitted that IP had not stopped him offending. He described having shoplifted on one occasion since being on the project, but did stress that IP had stopped him committing more serious offences.

Respondents were asked how they would change the project if they were running it. In response, the offenders who had been most positive about their experience of IP suggested that the IP phase of the order could be longer – or at least more flexible, so that those who wanted more help could receive it. It was also suggested that more project workers should be employed so that they could spend longer with each offender. Three respondents suggested that there could be more activities, and one suggested getting rid of the group work. Another offender thought that probation officers, rather than project workers should work on the scheme, and that there should be more discussion of offending behaviour and visits to prison for those who had not experienced custody.

Cost effectiveness

It is particularly difficult to assess the cost-effectiveness of a scheme during the first two years of its operation. Inevitably, there are costs associated with setting up a scheme that should be considered separately from the cost of running a scheme. However, even when operational, one would not expect a new project to be functioning at its optimum level in the first year. Magistrates need not only to be aware of the project in order to use it: they need to have trust in the scheme and the supervision that offenders will receive. Probation officers also need to be "won over" in order to ensure that sufficient referrals are made to make a scheme a financially viable one. Such matters should therefore be borne in mind in addressing the issue of the cost-effectiveness of the Gate Project.

During the study period, three Home Office grants were secured to fund the scheme. The first grant of just over £50,000 was ear-marked for the period January to December 1990, which included the setting-up of the project over January to May. The second grant for the same sum covered the period January 1991 to December 1991 and the third grant for £60,000 covered the third year. In addition, DTE raised £10-20,000 from charitable sources in each year to add to the Home Office grant.

In assessing the costs of the scheme, it should be emphasised that such estimates are inevitably approximate. The following table shows only the readily-calculated costs. It does not include the cost of senior probation service management input or the cost of normal probation supervision during the intensive phase of the order and thereafter (this will be considered below). The following costs should therefore be viewed as the price of the intensive component of intensive probation in Durham.

Table 4.20
Costs of Durham IP

Type of cost	Period			
	Jan 1990 to May 1990		June 1990 to May 1991	
	£	%	£	%
Staffing (DPS)	7,917	(32)	19,000	(22)
Staffing (DTE)	5,701	(23)	48,456	(56)
Running costs	8,619	(34)	11,285	(13)
Management fee	2,814	(11)	7,451	(9)
Total	25,051	(100)	86,192	(100)

Table 4.20 shows that during the setting up of the scheme over January to May 1990, £25,051 was spent, with over a third of this sum being accounted for by "running costs". These actually included £4,700 spent on renovation work on the office and the purchasing of office equipment. The scheme was actually ready to take referrals in June 1990. Costs for the first year are also shown in Table 4.20. Once the scheme was operating, the largest expense by far was staffing costs – amounting to 77 per cent of the total cost. The proportion of money spent on running costs was greatly decreased once the scheme was operating. The management fee in each period is that charged by DTE. This sum averaged as £560 per month during the setting up of the scheme and £620 per month in the first year.

The monitoring exercise showed that 20 IP orders were commenced in the first year. The large majority of these offenders would have completed the intensive phase of their orders over this period, as the intensive phase of the order lasted on average four and a half months. An estimate of the cost per order can therefore be calculated by dividing the cost of running the scheme for the first year by the number of orders made. This produces a figure of £4,300 per order.

It has already been pointed out that the first few years of a new project are likely to be the most expensive. Unfortunately the same detailed figures for the second full year of operation are not available. The figures in Table 4.20 were calculated by the project managers as part of an application to the Home Office for further funding and this process did not need to be repeated for the final grant. However, costs for the second year were probably very similar to those incurred in the first year. There were 25 orders made between June 1991 and the end of March 1992 (the termination date of the monitoring). If orders continued to be made at this rate, there would have been 30 orders commenced in the second year. Thus, the average cost of an order must have decreased significantly in the second year – to around £2,900, if costs remained at the same level.

An additional cost to those shown in Table 4.20, is the price of regular probation supervision over the intensive period of the order. The average annual cost of probation supervision over the year 1990/91 was estimated at £1,060 (Home Office 1990). Calculating the proportion of this sum for four and a half months of supervision gives a figure of £398. Adding this sum to the costs calculated above gives a first year cost of £4,698 and a second year cost of £3,298 for the intensive supervision component of IP. On top of these costs is the price of regular probation supervision over the rest of the order. The average total length of probation orders with IP requirements was 17.5 months. Subtracting the average period of four and a half months intensive supervision gives 13 extra months supervision at a cost of £1,148. Adding this sum to the costs of intensive supervision results in total costs of £5,846 for the first year and £4,446 for the second.

How does this compare with other disposals? According to prison statistics, the average weekly cost of imprisonment is £386 (Home Office 1991). This is considerably more expensive than the weekly cost of intensive supervision, which works out at an average of £260 for the first year of operation and £180 for the second year. The weekly cost of the order as a whole, including the long period of regular probation supervision, is considerably less than this. However such a comparison does not take account of the relative lengths of IP orders and imprisonment. The average length of an IP order is approximately four and a half months: how long would a comparable offender spend in custody? Of course, this question is impossible to answer accurately, but the sample of offenders who were accepted by the scheme and given custodial sentences could be taken as a comparison group. They were sentenced to an average of 20 months. If they served half of their sentences actually in custody, this would produce an average cost of £16,540 – far higher than the estimated total cost of an IP order. However, it could be argued that those accepted by the scheme but imprisoned are not a comparable group: most of these cases appeared at the Crown court and were at very high risk of custody. Nevertheless, even if the period spent in custody is halved, IP remains a much cheaper disposal: a prisoner serving five months in custody costs the state £8,270.

Compared with imprisonment, IP appears to be cheap. However, comparison with probation or community service shows IP to be a very expensive community disposal. As has been cited, probation statistics calculate the average cost of a year's probation supervision as being in the region of £1,060. The same source gives the average cost for a CSO as £1,020.

Ideally, one would want to assess cost-effectiveness not only in terms of the positive savings from diversion from custody but the negative costs of reoffending. This issue cannot be addressed until more reoffending information is available. Ignoring the price of reconvictions for the present, what can be said is that IP is cost-effective to the extent that it replaces prison sentences and operates as an alternative to custody. Information from the monitoring and interviews shows quite convincingly that offenders given an IP order were at considerable risk of custody.

Conclusions

By and large, the IP in Durham was implemented and developed according to plan. A key factor in the successful implementation of the scheme was the early and prolonged negotiations with the local NAPO branch, which allowed the scheme to be almost universally accepted amongst the field teams. Inevitably, as with any new idea – and especially one proceeding from the Home Office involving voluntary sector partnership and out-reach work – there was initial scepticism and some resistance. However, through a combination of preparatory negotiations, public relations work and, perhaps, a comparatively receptive political environment, intensive probation was accepted by the majority of probation officers as a useful new provision for high tariff offenders.

A considerable effort was also made by IP staff to explain to probation officers the purpose and function of the scheme. The Gate Project needed to overcome a certain amount of protectionism from day centre staff and probation officers closely allied with the day centres. Inevitably, there were early suspicions in certain quarters that the advent of a new, high tariff, intensive probation order would mean competition for day centre cases. Perhaps these fears were never completely dispelled, but extensive discussions and a detailed description of the differences between IP and day centre target groups certainly aided in the acceptance of the new project.

The monitoring and interview data show quite convincingly that the scheme has also been successful in targeting referrals at considerable risk of custody. Analysis of previous criminal history and risk of custody data for those who actually received IP shows them to be more similar to offenders given custody than those given 4A/4B orders. The opinions of project staff, SPOs, probation officers and offenders bear out this finding, with IP repeatedly described as a direct alternative to custody: the 'last resort' among community penalties.

This is not to say that there have not been difficulties: any new scheme encounters teething problems and needs to have the flexibility to make slight changes of direction. One early participant in the scheme was arrested towards the end of the IP phase of his order and was subsequently convicted of a number of offences committed while he had been on the project. His project worker had put a lot of effort into trying to help him with his various problems, and his reoffending caused some disillusionment. However, this seems to have formed part of an inevitable learning process: at first there was a very high degree of optimism and ambition. It was perhaps unavoidable that some hopes were dashed. The experience does not seem to have adversely affected morale on the project in the long run – project workers seemed to derive a high degree of job satisfaction from working closely with offenders in this way.

There were also some early problems with the management of the project. This may have been due to a degree of ambivalence in certain sections of the service towards working with the voluntary sector. However, these problems did seem to be resolved. The managers of the project were also able to learn from the failures on IP. A change that resulted from this process was the new focus on the importance of self-motivation in targeting offenders for IP.

Although only eleven of the 45 offenders given IP orders were interviewed, some very interesting issues emerged from the exercise. Highly positive views were expressed about the project workers: they were not seen as controlling or intrusive, on the contrary they were perceived primarily as helpers. Out-reach work contributed to this perspective, as project workers were able to be flexible and reactive to offenders' needs. When offenders were asked to compare project workers with probation officers, many described their relationships with project workers as more friendly and informal. There are a number of possible explanations for this: unlike probation officers, project workers do not have the power to breach offenders, and this may lead to less formal relationships. Project workers are also able to spend a lot more of the time with offenders, not having the same office-bound administrative duties as probation officers. Finally, according to the offenders interviewed, an important factor is that most of the contact occurred outside the formal environment of the probation office. Of course, there are also disadvantages to the project worker approach to supervision. It might be conjectured that without some formal distance in the relationship between project worker and offender, it might be difficult for project workers to report unacceptable behaviour to the responsible probation officer. There is also the problem that some offenders on IP were in danger of becoming dependent on their project workers. This could create problems when they went on to "normal" supervision.

In summary, the Durham Intensive Probation Project appears to have been successful in terms of implementation and diversion of offenders from custody. It has also been successful in showing that intensive out-reach work can be an effective way of dealing with the welfare needs of offenders, and yet not be perceived as intrusive. Whether or not this has been associated with a diminution in offending behaviour remains to be seen. A future report will compare the recidivism and breach rates for the IP and 4A/4B samples in this study.

5 Intensive Probation in West Yorkshire (Leeds)

Introduction

West Yorkshire Probation Service ran two intensive probation programmes in Leeds, both of which were studied. One, the Leeds Intensive Supervision Project (LISP) was entirely a probation service project, while the other, the Edge, was run in partnership with a voluntary body. Overall, work done with offenders was similar in both schemes. The schemes differed, however, in their development, the structure of each organisation and their staff, in the referral process of each and in their underlying philosophies.

The projects evolved in different ways: LISP was based on a previous scheme while the Edge started from scratch. In fact, LISP was the product of several converging developments. During 1983/84, the Save the Children Fund became interested in the Massachusetts Initiative, a tracking scheme which was developed in the United States in the early 1970s, and, using money from the Intermediate Treatment budget, they set up a tracking package for juveniles. During the same period, the maingrade probation team at Seacroft – one problem area in Leeds with very high levels of custodial disposals for young offenders – began experimenting with tracking as a way of addressing this problem as, at that time, there were no 4A or 4B disposals available in the area. They imported the initiative from Halifax where a small adult scheme was in operation. Management had seen the operation of the scheme for juveniles and bid for money to set up an adult scheme which came through in 1985. The Seacroft team seemed to be the best placed to carry the scheme through and tracking for adult offenders was formally initiated there. A Senior Probation Officer in project development was asked to coordinate it.

At this time, tracking involved three field teams and one team of eight part-time trackers. The trackers were not qualified probation officers but had been trained by the team. Each tracker made 60 contacts with the offender assigned to him/her over a period of 13 weeks, for six days a week. This attracted considerable opposition from NAPO and was resisted by a number of probation officers. The issue became extremely heated for a time, the SPO was moved off the programme and in the latter half of the 1980s the scheme became very isolated (and was confused with the "tagging" debate). In 1988, however, management's interest in a refined version of tracking was renewed following the government's new emphasis on reducing the prison population through alternatives to custody. The original SPO was reinstated and, in 1989, concerted efforts were made to develop tracking into IP and to resolve differences between those who operated the scheme and the local branch of NAPO.

The Edge project had a rather different history, developing from scratch rather than evolving from another project. In late 1987, senior probation managers in Leeds were concerned about the number of 17-20 year olds going into custody. Tracking, which had not yet developed into LISP, was operating in the Seacroft, York Road and West Leeds teams but was not available on a city-wide basis. Senior management at area level liaised with the National Children's Home (NCH) and, with the publication of *Punishment, Custody and the Community* (Home Office, 1988a), it became apparent that the extra funding needed to cover the city might become available. A steering group was set up representing the two bodies and a city-wide programme targeting 17-20 year olds was then put forward and accepted, with LISP agreeing to move away from the 17-20 year old age group. Because it was a new and separate scheme from LISP, an extra effort was made to sell it to the magistrates and judges. This included presentations and visits to the project.

Initially, the Edge project also met with some resistance from probation staff in Leeds who felt that it had been parachuted in on them from above, and who were not happy about what they saw as a lack of consultation about forming a partnership with a voluntary body. It was felt that the extra resources from the government should have been directed at the probation service, which had greater experience in dealing with offenders, rather than a voluntary body. This time, however, the management group drew on their experience with tracking and liaised with maingrade staff on drafting principles and practice guidelines for the project. Partly because of this, and partly because it was seen as having a 'softer', less controlling profile, the Edge project was received more readily by probation officers than its counterpart.

It was also at this time that NAPO put pressure on probation management to bring LISP into line with the principles set out for the Edge which they deemed acceptable for an alternative to custody for young offenders. In fact, the former had changed considerably over the years from a fixed, six-contacts-a-week intervention into a scheme with far greater emphasis on the individual's needs, as well as the protection of the public which had always been a significant part of their philosophy. Thus, in practice, the two programmes were not essentially different, but it was felt necessary for all concerned to sit down and rewrite some of LISP's guidelines to bring it into line with the overall service strategy. When NAPO was satisfied with the final product (at the beginning of 1990), the extra post needed to extend LISP city-wide was granted and the post was filled shortly afterwards.

Initially, therefore, the two programmes were different in that they addressed different age groups, one developed from a previous (and contentious) project (tracking) while the other developed independently, and one was run internally while the other operated in partnership with a voluntary body. The programmes were similar in that both addressed the needs of the individual whilst acknowledging the need for public safety and, given that IP was aimed at very high tariff offenders, both programmes targetted principally the Crown court. The aim of both projects was to reduce custodial disposals by providing alternative, high tariff community disposals and to reduce reoffending while on the programmes.

Both projects monitored information on referrals made and produced annual reports. In addition, the Edge project was studied by researchers at Leeds University who focused on assessing the effectiveness of its targeting.

What IP entailed in Leeds

As noted above, there were some similarities, as well as differences, between the two Leeds IP schemes in their origins and objectives. In this part of the report the question of how similar the schemes were is looked at in more detail while considering the practical aspects of the schemes.

Structure and staffing

The Edge project was based in a house in Leeds city centre provided by NCH. It consisted of a project manager, an administrator, and five project workers who worked directly with field probation officers. The project was overseen by a management group comprising the project manager, the ACPO and SPO responsible for Replacements to Custody initiatives and a Principal Officer of National Children's Homes (NCH), and was chaired by a Leeds magistrate who was also a member of the West Yorkshire Probation Committee.

LISP was located in the Replacements to Custody unit at the probation office in Leeds city centre. It was supervised by a senior probation officer and included two probation officers who ran the scheme on a day to day basis (a third was later added) and a team of eight programme workers, of whom five worked full-time and three worked part-time. It was structurally different to the Edge in that the programme workers did not work directly with field officers; they were supervised by the LISP probation officers who in turn liaised with the field officers and processed referrals. For this reason they were referred to as 'probation liaison officers'. NAPO had expressed concern over the extra tier of probation officers in LISP on the grounds that it was not clear whether it was the field probation officers or the LISP probation officers who were 'driving' the probation order.

The backgrounds of the project/programme workers also differed. Three of the Edge project workers had social work or youth work backgrounds, one had a legal and training background and one was an ex-police officer who had also worked in education welfare. Two members of the team had previously worked for LACCS (Leeds Alternative to Care and Custody Scheme), the juvenile alternatives scheme managed by the Social Services Department. Unlike the Edge, none of the programme workers at LISP had professional social work backgrounds and all were probation service assistants: two were ex-police officers, one was an ex-bar worker, one was an engineer and voluntary community worker, one was an ex-priest, one was a dancer and one a psychiatric nurse. This was a deliberate decision based on a belief in the merits of involving members of the community in work with offenders.

The backgrounds of the LISP programme workers initially caused concern among some maingrade officers who felt that unqualified people were being recruited to do what, essentially, was probation work. At LISP, the recruiting senior probation officer was looking for a belief in the potential for change in others, the ability to get on with the probation officer as well as the offender, to use authority appropriately and to understand the boundaries of the role. As part of the selection process, potential programme workers received a presentation from experienced programme workers and underwent an induction period during which they would shadow the experienced programme worker.

It could be said that both organisations therefore had three tiers of management, each with a senior probation officer either managing the project or on the project committee. The third tier at each was staffed by programme/project workers who had not had probation experience, but, in the case of the Edge, several had social work backgrounds. The organisations differed in the second tier which, at the Edge, was staffed by an NCH worker, but which, at LISP, was staffed by two probation officers in the role of probation liaison officers. It is interesting to note that while NAPO initially voiced concern over the professionalism of the LISP programme workers, field probation officers later criticised some of the Edge workers for not being as professional in court as LISP's probation liaison officers (see Views of Probation Officers).

The referral process

Referrals to both projects were made by the field probation officer. Guided by the nature of the offence, the circumstances surrounding it, the offender's risk of custody (assessed using the Cambridgeshire Risk of Custody scale) and his/her motivation, the probation officer would make a decision about the person's suitability for intensive supervision in the community. A referral was made in either of two ways. Firstly, the probation officer could ring and make the referral over the phone before the offender's first court appearance, which allowed an assessment of suitability before going to court. Secondly, the probation officer could make a referral to either programme in court and, if the judge or magistrates agreed, the defendant was either held on remand or bailed while an assessment took place. If access was granted to a defendant held on remand, an interview would take place where motivation to change and commitment to the programme were assessed.

Bail assessment was only possible at LISP and could take one of two forms, voluntary participation or conditional bail assessment, both of which involved the court granting bail at the probation liaison officer's request. Voluntary participation requested that the defendant participate for an unspecified amount of time in intensive supervision. Conditional bail consisted of 28 days bail, usually given to people who would otherwise be remanded in custody. At the end of the bail period, the probation liaison officer would go back to court to say whether the person was suitable or not. Conditional bail assessment was not popular with NAPO who were concerned that people who were given conditional bail might be having strings attached unnecessarily, especially since the Edge did not operate such a system and was content to assess people while they were remanded in custody.

If the offender was deemed suitable and motivated following assessment or, in the case of the Edge, discussion at the team meeting, a detailed report was drafted and submitted at court with the individual's SIR. This contained a summary of the person's background and offending history, outlined why it was felt that he/she might be suitable for supervision in the community, and identified the particular problems that would be addressed during supervision should the referral be successful. In the case of the Edge project, the project worker assigned to the case attended the court in case any queries were raised by the sentencer. In the case of LISP, this was done by one of the probation liaison officers.

A double-gatekeeping system therefore operated for referrals to both projects: once a defendant had been referred for IP, they would be assessed for suitability at LISP by a probation liaison officer or, at the Edge, at a meeting of the manager and the project workers. If the person was thought not to be at high risk of custody a lower tariff community disposal (such as community service or an attendance centre) would be recommended by the report writer instead in order to keep IP at an appropriately high tariff position.

Interpretation of the order

IP at Leeds generally involved a 60 day 4A requirement alongside a probation order of usually 18 months or two years. How these 60 days of IP were operationalised varied considerably between the Edge and LISP.

IP at the Edge

The Edge interpreted the 60 day order in terms of a two month individualised programme for each participant. Although the emphasis of the programme could be different for each individual, problems with accommodation, employment, relationships, alcohol and drug dependency were all common. The starting point for the Edge project worker and the participant was to draw up an agreed statement of specific aims and objectives to be achieved during the eight weeks. Their particular needs and problems would have been identified during the assessment phase and a timetable would be drawn up in order to address these.

In parallel with the individualised programme, the Edge ran sessions challenging offending behaviour, emphasising the value of mediation with victims wherever possible. The Edge project workers, in common with those at LISP, had several housing and accommodation contacts, including Timble, an organisation funded partly by the probation service focusing on single homeless people. For both the Edge and LISP, help with employment usually came in the shape of a government employment training (ET) scheme which varied enormously in quality. Project workers, however, made a concerted effort to support and encourage IP participants to be assertive and gain a place on a scheme which they had chosen, rather than were merely assigned to.

The programme usually began with four sessions a week with the project worker for the first fortnight. Frequency of contact was then reduced depending on the participant's needs and progress. Sessions were always one-to-one; no groupwork was involved. Offenders would also have higher than usual contact with their probation officer – at least once a week – who was kept informed by the project worker of the participant's progress. Two review meetings involving the participant, the project worker and the probation officer also took place, the first after a month had elapsed and the second at the end of the programme.

IP at LISP

IP at LISP was much longer than at the Edge. Here, a 60 day order was interpreted in the form of 60 contacts (each contact counting as a 'day') usually spread over a six month period. Initial assessment and report presentation at court was quite similar to that of the Edge, although in court, if the judge agreed, the offender underwent a period of 'assessment in the community'.

An essential difference between IP at LISP and at the Edge was that, from the beginning of the order, the work at LISP involved a daily programme which was agreed between the programme worker and the offender. Each day, offenders would plan their activities for the next 24 hours so that the programme worker could help them to think ahead and avoid situations in which they were at risk of offending. If the programme worker was concerned that the offender might be at risk of offending, he/she would state that an unannounced visit might be made within a period of a few days, as an extra check. As a result of the agreed daily programme, the probation liaison officers felt some confidence telling the court that they knew where their offenders were at any time and that they were less at risk. It was this aspect of the LISP programme which contributed to management's view of LISP as taking more account of public protection than the Edge project.

Incorporated into the daily programme was the offender's individual plan which addressed problem areas identified during assessment. In this sense, the nature of the contact between offender and programme worker was very similar for both the Edge and LISP, although LISP spread it over a longer period. As with the Edge, all work with the offenders was carried out on a one-to-one basis. Contact was very high over the first few weeks, usually with as many as five or six meetings a week depending on the needs of each case and the risk. All offenders had the phone numbers of their workers and other staff for help if a crisis occurred, or to make changes in their daily programme.

INTENSIVE PROBATION IN WEST YORKSHIRE (LEEDS)

During the intensive part of the order, the offender would see his/her probation officer once a week. A three-way meeting between the offender, programme worker and field probation officer usually took place once a fortnight, plus monthly reviews where the probation liaison officer was included. The programme worker kept in regular telephone contact with the probation officer throughout IP. At the end of the six month period, a final review meeting would take place. This involved the offender, the programme worker, the field probation officer, a probation liaison officer and a magistrate (one of those who originally heard the case in court, where possible). The purpose of the final review was to discuss the general progress of the offender, along with any achievements and/or difficulties or breaches which occurred and to wish the individual luck in the remaining part of their order. It also provided useful feedback for the magistrate.

Because of the intensity of both the Edge programme and LISP in terms of contact with the project worker, and bearing in mind that this may be the closest supervision that the IP offender had experienced in his or her life, it was possible that problems of disengagement could occur at the end of the IP order if the offender had grown to be too dependent on the project worker. However, project workers and those supervising them said that this was often more of a problem for them than for the offender and if the project worker was trained properly, problems did not arise. Project workers were trained to 'let go' of their offenders and this was aided by a 'weaning off' phase in the final few weeks of the programme during which contact was reduced at both the Edge and at LISP.

Both projects had very clear breach proceedings stated in their practice guidelines. If the offender did not comply with the conditions of the order, the probation liaison officer in consultation with the field probation officer invoked a three stage breach process where the third stage depended on the nature of the breach. They would first issue a verbal warning, then a written warning, followed by a possible return to court with either the recommendation of a warning or a recommendation that the IP condition be revoked. In practice, the number of warnings or breach proceedings would depend on the response of the offender and his/her risk to the public. The Edge stated very similar practice guidelines in the case of breaches.

Referrals for IP

As well as being studied by the Research and Planning Unit (along with LISP), the Edge project was monitored separately by the Centre for Criminal Justice Studies at Leeds University. This study (Brownlee and Joanes, 1992) focused on the Edge project from its inception and compared those sentenced to IP at the Edge, those referred for IP but sentenced to custody, and a sample of those sentenced to custody but who were not referred for IP. Where relevant, reference is made to Brownlee and Joanes's main findings. Where comparisons are made, it should be borne in mind that, unless specified otherwise, Brownlee and Joanes's figures refer to data collected over three years and ending in March 1992. Furthermore, their referral figures only included those which either resulted in a probation order with a condition to attend the project or a custodial sentence; the RPU figures, on the other hand, included all referrals whatever the outcome.

In this section, data from the two projects are considered together to give an overall picture of IP in West Yorkshire. However, it should be borne in mind that the figures are not strictly comparable since the projects targeted different age groups. The age differences may be expected, to some extent, to account for differences in criminal history.

Demographic information

Between 1st April 1990 and 31st March 1992, a total of 532 referrals were made to IP projects in Leeds: 233 to the Edge and 299 to LISP. Brownlee and Joanes recorded 187 referrals to the Edge over the same period. Nearly all referrals were male (97 per cent at the Edge and 96 per cent at LISP).

The majority of referrals were white (88 per cent at the Edge and 94 per cent at LISP). Of the 27 remaining cases at the Edge, 12 were categorised as Black-Other, four as Black-Caribbean, one as Black-African, two as Pakistani, one as Indian, one as Bangladeshi and six as Other. Of the remaining 21 cases at LISP, seven were categorised as Black-Caribbean, seven as Black-Other, two as Indian, two as Other and one as Black-African. There was no information for two cases at LISP.

A similarly high proportion of referrals to both projects were unemployed (82 per cent at the Edge and 81 per cent at LISP). At the Edge, 15 per cent were working and three per cent on government training schemes. At LISP, 18 per cent were employed and one per cent on government training schemes.

Because the projects targeted different age ranges, the age distributions at each were quite different. At the Edge, ages ranged between 17 and 21: nine per cent were 17, 31 per cent 18 and roughly one quarter each were 19 and 20. The ten per cent aged 21 fell beyond the intended age limits for this project. However, this could have been due to the fact that, for the purpose of this research, an offender's age was calculated from the year of referral rather than from the exact date of referral. Furthermore, some offenders may have been 20 years old when referred to the Edge, but 21 when convicted or when beginning an IP order.

Referrals to LISP were much older, with ages ranging between 17 and 55 years old. Thirty-one referrals (11 per cent) were under 21 and therefore fell outside the target age bracket (aged 21 and over). These had often been referred initially to the Edge project and were only taken by LISP because the Edge was full. Fifty-one per cent were in the age group 21-25 and 19 per cent in the age group 26-30.

INTENSIVE PROBATION IN WEST YORKSHIRE (LEEDS)

Seriousness of referrals

The main aim of the intensive probation projects in West Yorkshire was to provide an alternative to custody for high tariff offenders, that is, those most likely to receive custodial sentences. The gatekeeping procedures described above were devised in order to identify characteristics of individual offenders which would suggest that they were high risk cases. In general, referrals were expected to have at least one of the following characteristics: a high Risk of Custody score, a Crown Court appearance, a high number of previous convictions and previous experience of custody (via a conviction or remand in custody in respect of the current charge). Table 5.1 shows the Risk of Custody scores of referrals to each project.

Table 5.1
Risk of Custody scores

	Edge		LISP	
Score (%)	n	%	n	%
0-50	24	(11)	21	(7)
51-70	20	(10)	16	(6)
71-99	86	(41)	143	(49)
100	80	(38)	114	(39)
Total[1]	210	(100)	294	(100)

[1] Information was unavailable for 23 referrals to the Edge and 5 at LISP.

As can be seen, more than a third in each group scored the maximum of 100 per cent and the majority of referrals to each scored more than 70 per cent.

A high proportion of referrals to each project were made via the Crown Court: 71 per cent at the Edge and 75 per cent at LISP.

The two projects differed with respect to the number of previous convictions of referrals and this is largely a reflection of the age-ranges of the projects. Eleven per cent of referrals to the Edge had no previous convictions and less than one-third had more than five (29 per cent). At LISP, only three per cent had no previous convictions while two-thirds had more than five (66 per cent).

Table 5.2
Number of previous convictions

Number	Edge		LISP	
	n	%	n	%
None	26	(11)	10	(3)
1 to 5	140	(60)	91	(30)
6 to 10	53	(23)	95	(32)
11 to 15	12	(5)	60	(20)
16+	2	(1)	43	(14)
Total[1]	233	(100)	299	(100)

[1] Information was unavailable for 1 referral at the Edge.

As already noted, one indicator of the likelihood of a custodial sentence being passed was past experience of custody, either in the form of a previous sentence or where a defendant was currently remanded in custody. Information on the most serious previous disposal (Table 5.3) shows that more than a third (36 per cent) of those referred to the Edge had had previous custodial sentences; as might be expected this was almost exclusively in a Young Offender Institution. This figure was twice as high at LISP where three-quarters (75 per cent) had past experience of custody, more than half of these having been in prison. Again, this difference between the two projects is largely a reflection of the target age range.

Information on IP referrals' most serious previous offence reveals that half the Edge referrals (48 per cent) and around two-thirds of LISP referrals (62 per cent) had previously been convicted of a serious offence, i.e. violence, sexual offences, robbery or burglary in a dwelling. At the Edge, these were predominantly burglaries in a dwelling (28 per cent), violence (14 per cent), robbery (five per cent) and sexual offences (one per cent). At LISP, the most serious previous offences included violence (41 per cent), burglary in a dwelling (11 per cent), robbery (seven per cent) and sexual offences (two per cent).

Fifty-seven per cent of the Edge referrals and 50 per cent of LISP referrals had been remanded in custody before sentence. At the Edge, 44 per cent had been remanded for the whole period and 13 per cent with a period on bail. Of the LISP referrals, 46 per cent had been remanded in custody for the whole period and four per cent with a period on bail.

Table 5.3
Most serious previous disposal

	Edge		LISP	
Disposal	n	%	n	%
No Previous Disposal	26	(11)	10	(3)
Prison	1	-	118	(40)
Young Offender Institution	83	(36)	104	(35)
Wholly Suspended Sentence	-	-	14	(5)
Probation+4A/4B	8	(3)	6	(2)
Probation+Hostel Requirement	2	(1)	2	(1)
Community Service	37	(16)	14	(5)
Probation	47	(20)	16	(5)
Attendance Centre	9	(4)	5	(2)
Fine/Compensation	10	(4)	6	(2)
Discharge	5	(2)	1	-
Other	4	(2)	3	(1)
Total[1]	232	(100)	299	(100)

[1] Information was unavailable for 1 referral at the Edge.

Table 5.4 shows the main offence for which offenders were referred to each project. At the Edge, more than half (52 per cent) were charged with a serious offence compared to 43 per cent at LISP. As can be seen, a high proportion of referrals to the Edge had been charged with burglary either in a dwelling or a non-dwelling: 51 per cent compared to 41 per cent at LISP; furthermore, referrals to the Edge were twice as likely to have been charged with robbery. Referrals to LISP, on the other hand, were more likely to have been charged with theft/handling and violence.

Table 5.4
Main offence at the time of referral

Offence	Edge		LISP	
	n	%	n	%
Violence	25	(11)	42	(14)
Sex Offence	1	-	2	(1)
Robbery	26	(11)	17	(6)
Burglary (in a dwelling)	69	(30)	67	(22)
Burglary (in a non-dwelling)	48	(21)	56	(19)
Theft/Handling	19	(8)	58	(19)
TWOC/TADA	16	(7)	15	(5)
Fraud/Forgery	1	-	9	(3)
Drugs	-	-	5	(2)
Criminal Damage	1	-	1	-
Public Order	2	-	-	-
Indictable Motoring	14	(6)	20	(7)
Breach/Non-Payment Of Fine	2	(1)	3	(1)
Other	9	(4)	4	(1)
Total	233	(100)	299	(100)

Most referrals to both projects had additional offences with which they were being charged at the time of referral (81 per cent at the Edge and 82 per cent at LISP). At the Edge, 28 per cent had more than five such offences while at LISP, 18 per cent had more than five such offences.

As has already been noted, the majority of those referred to both projects had previous convictions. Including those for whom the present offence was the first, i.e. those with no previous convictions, the average age at first conviction was 15 years old at the Edge and 16 years at LISP.

From referral to sentence

In court, practically all referrals pleaded guilty to one or all of the offences they had been charged with (99 per cent at both projects). Of those referred for an IP assessment, the majority had been recommended for IP in their SIR, either on its own or in addition to other recommendations (84 per cent at the Edge and 64 per cent at LISP) (see Table 5.5).

Table 5.5
SIR recommendations

Recommended sentence	Edge		LISP	
	n	%	n	%
IP	156	(78)	180	(62)
IP+Other(s)	12	(6)	6	(2)
CSO	7	(4)	22	(8)
4A/4B	1	-	9	(3)
Probation	17	(8)	35	(12)
Custody	-	-	1	-
Fine	-	-	2	(1)
Discharge	-	-	1	-
Other	7	(4)	21	(7)
No recommendation	-	-	12	(4)
No SIR	1	-	2	(1)
Total[1]	201	(100)	291	(100)

[1] Information was unavailable for 32 referrals to the Edge and 8 to LISP.

All referrals were assessed by the project workers at the Edge and by the probation liaison officers at LISP. More than three-quarters of the Edge referrals (78 per cent) were deemed suitable for the programme compared to 56 per cent at LISP (this difference may reflect either more suitable referrals made to the Edge or tighter gatekeeping on the part of LISP). However, where IP was recommended by the probation officer, 96 per cent of cases at the Edge and 84 per cent at LISP were considered suitable. This indicates a high degree of congruence between probation officers' views of how suitable a person may be for IP and their suitability as judged by the probation liaison officers at LISP and, particularly, the team of project workers at the Edge. Five referrals to LISP were not assessed because the court had refused to adjourn for an assessment. The most common reason for rejection by staff at both projects was that the individual was not considered to be at high enough risk of custody to benefit from the programme. Another common reason was that the individual concerned was judged to be unsuitable for the programme; he/she was assessed as lacking motivation, unwilling to co-operate, or simply not interested in doing IP.

Of the 532 referrals for IP, 200 (42 per cent) were sentenced to IP. Although more referrals were made to LISP, a greater proportion of those sentenced to IP had been referred to the Edge: 57 per cent of referrals to the Edge (107 offenders) were sentenced to IP compared to 32 per cent of referrals to LISP (93 offenders).

Nearly three-quarters of those sentenced to IP were sentenced in the Crown Court (71 per cent), 71 per cent of Edge referrals and 75 per cent of LISP referrals.

The Crown Court and magistrates' courts were similar in the proportion of referrals who were actually sentenced to IP at each: 42 per cent of referrals to the Crown Court received IP compared to 44 per cent of referrals to magistrates' courts. This was lower than the figures recorded by Brownlee and Joanes which, nonetheless, were comparable at 57 and 56 per cent respectively. Further examination of the data shows that, where IP was recommended on the SIR, IP was given by the court in 58 per cent of cases.

Table 5.6 sets out the court disposals for referrals to each project. Although 205 offenders were sentenced to a probation order with a 4A requirement, only 196 of these were IP orders. One probation order with a hostel requirement was actually an IP order, and the legal status of the three remaining IP orders was not known.

Overall, 42 per cent of referrals – the same proportion as those who received IP – received a custodial sentence. The mean length of custody was just under two years (22 months).

Table 5.6
Court disposal

Disposal	Edge		LISP	
	n	%	n	%
Prison	-	-	124	(42)
Young Offender Institution	70	(34)	16	(5)
Partially Suspended Sentence	-	-	3	(1)
Wholly Suspended Sentence	-	-	9	(3)
Probation+4A	106	(52)	99	(34)
Probation+Hostel Requirement	2	(1)	1	-
Community Service	9	(4)	14	(5)
Probation	14	(7)	21	(7)
Attendance Centre	1	-	1	-
Fine/Compensation	2	(1)	3	(1)
Discharge	-	-	1	-
Other	2	(1)	2	(1)
Total[1]	206	(100)	294	(100)

[1] Information was unavailable for 27 referrals to the Edge and 5 to LISP.

INTENSIVE PROBATION IN WEST YORKSHIRE (LEEDS)

As mentioned above, a more detailed breakdown of the figures for the Edge can be found in Brownlee and Joanes's report which also includes preliminary figures on reconviction rates.

The comparison group: community service orders

At the same time as IP referrals were being monitored, data were also collected on all those in Leeds who were sentenced to community service between 1 April 1990 and 31 March 1992. This was intended to provide a comparison group to see whether those sentenced to IP were at greater risk of custody than those who received CS.

A total of 653 offenders received CS during this period. Thirty-nine per cent were aged 17-20, 31 per cent were aged 21-25 and nine per cent were over 35 years old. Practically all (96 per cent) were male and the ethnic group of the majority (86 per cent) was white with the remaining 14 per cent classified as either Black-Afro-Caribbean, Black-Other, Asian or Other. Nearly two-thirds (60 per cent) were unemployed, with most of the rest (34 per cent) in employment. This is a much higher proportion than for those who were referred for IP.

Nineteen per cent had Risk of Custody scores of more than 80 on the Cambridgeshire scale. Exactly half appeared at Crown Court and half appeared at magistrates' court. Twenty-six per cent had no previous convictions and 24 per cent had more than five. Less than a quarter (23 per cent) had past experience of custody and almost all (94 per cent) were on bail before appearing in court.

Less than a quarter (21 per cent) of offences for which the CS group were sentenced were serious, i.e. violence, a sex offence, robbery or burglary in a dwelling. Two-thirds (66 per cent) had been charged with additional offences, but only 5 per cent with more than five.

Two-thirds (67 per cent) had been recommended community service in their SIR. Seven had been recommended for IP. All 653 were sentenced to community service. The length of the community service orders ranged between 120 and 240 hours, with a mean length of 150 hours.

These figures show that those getting CS appeared to be less serious offenders than those referred for IP, in that fewer had high Risk of Custody scores, a previous custodial sentence, a high number of previous convictions or a serious current offence. Since the comparison group consisted of offenders who had already been sentenced, however, a more detailed comparison can be made between the CS group and those IP referrals who were actually sentenced to IP. The following comparison also includes IP referrals who received a custodial sentence.

Comparison of referral data

If IP was indeed being used as an alternative to custody, the community service group should be less serious than those sentenced to IP and, as far as possible, the scores of the IP group should be very similar to those referrals who were sentenced to custody.

The data confirm that in many respects the IP group was much closer to the custody group than to the CS group. Table 5.7 shows that the three groups were very similar both in age and in the fact that very few female offenders received either of these sentences. Interestingly, the community service group presented a higher proportion of offenders whose ethnic group was non-white than both the IP group and the custody group, which had the lowest proportion.

Table 5.7

Comparison of age, sex, ethnic group and employment status

	CS		IP		Custody	
	17-20	21+1	Edge	LISP	Edge	LISP
	(n=252)	(n=399)	(n=107)	(n=93)	(n=70)	(n=140)
Age range (years)	17-20	21-59	17-21	17-50	17-21	18-55
Mean age (years)	19	28	19	26	19	17
Per cent female	3%	4%	2%	3%	1%	3%
Per cent ethnic group is non-white	18%	12%	8%	10%	17%	4%
Per cent unemployed	63%	58%	88%	80%	74%	84%

However, Table 5.8 shows the IP group to be very similar to the custody group (but different from the CS group) in terms of their offending history: both had far more offenders with six or more previous convictions and very few offenders had no previous convictions. Although CS data on previous offences was not available, most of the IP and the custody groups had previously been convicted of a serious offence (violence, sex offence, robbery or house burglary). Most of the IP and custody groups had also had previous experience of a custodial sentence.

Table 5.8
Comparison of offending history

	CS		IP		Custody	
	17-20	*21+*	*Edge*	*LISP*	*Edge*	*LISP*
	(n=252)	*(n=399)*	*(n=107)*	*(n=93)*	*(n=70)*	*(n=140)*
Mean age at first conviction (years)	-	-	15	16	15	16
Mean number of previous convictions	2	6	4	9	4	10
Per cent with no previous convictions	34%	21%	10%	2%	9%	4%
Per cent with 6+ previous convictions	7%	37%	35%	70%	29%	69%
Per cent with serious previous offence	-	-	56%	62%	49%	65%
Per cent with previous custody	10%	32%	40%	78%	35%	79%

In terms of the current offence, the IP and custody groups contained twice as many people who had been charged with a serious offence (violence, sex offence, robbery or house burglary) as the CS group and were charged with more additional offences (see Table 5.9). As a result of this and the above factors, they scored very highly on the Cambridgeshire Risk of Custody scale.

Table 5.9
Comparison of current offence(s)

	CS		IP		Custody	
	17-20	*21+*	*Edge*	*LISP*	*Edge*	*LISP*
	(n=252)	*(n=399)*	*(n=107)*	*(n=93)*	*(n=70)*	*(n=140)*
Per cent with serious main offence	26%	19%	49%	58%	76%	50%
Mean number of other offences	2	1	5	4	4	3
Mean Risk of Custody score	49%	50%	86%	89%	90%	91%

Unlike the IP and custody groups, very few among the CS group had been remanded in custody immediately before the court appearance (Table 5.10). Most of the IP and custody groups had appeared at the Crown Court.

Table 5.10
Comparison of court information

	CS		IP		Custody	
	17-20	21+	Edge	LISP	Edge	LISP
	(n=252)	(n=399)	(n=107)	(n=93)	(n=70)	(n=140)
Per cent remanded in custody before trial	9%	4%	56%	54%	66%	56%
Per cent at Crown Court	56%	47%	69%	74%	85%	83%
Mean length of sentence	151 hrs	150 hrs	21mths	22mths	19mths	22mths

From a comparison of the monitoring data, therefore, it can be seen that the IP and custody groups were very similar to each other. This suggests that West Yorkshire Probation Service had accurately targeted high risk offenders for IP. Referrals generally had a high Risk of Custody score reflecting the fact that the current offence was serious, they had had several previous convictions and previous experience of custody. Only one referral was outside the target age group at the time of referral. Most referrals made were accepted onto the programme; however, only half were actually given IP by the court. Although not necessarily a favourable outcome, it is encouraging to note that those who did not get IP were given substantial custodial sentences, again suggesting that IP in West Yorkshire was being used as an alternative to custody.

Successful completions

Some outcome information has been received on 107 offenders sentenced to IP (54 per cent of the total number sentenced to IP) and 278 offenders sentenced to CS (43 per cent). Table 5.11 compares the outcome between the two groups. It can be seen that a higher proportion of offenders completed IP successfully than completed CS successfully, with more CS offenders being breached for non-compliance with the conditions of the order. This is very preliminary information and should be treated with caution; more details will be available in a later publication.

Table 5.11
Comparison of outcome data

	CS		IP	
	n	%	n	%
Completed sentence successfully	203	(76)	92	(86)
Terminated due to breach	26	(10)	1	(1)
Terminated due to reoffending	11	(4)	6	(6)
Terminated due to breach and reoffending	17	(6)	6	(6)
Terminated due to illness	5	(2)	-	-
Terminated due to other reason	5	(2)	2	(2)
Total[1]	267	(100)	107	(100)

[1] Information was unavailable for 389 CS cases and 90 IP cases.

Views of IP in Leeds

In addition to the use of monitoring data, this evaluation includes the views of sentencers, probation officers, senior managers and offenders who had been on the programme. The magistrates were sent a mail questionnaire in November 1990. Face-to-face interviews were carried out with all other respondents.

The views of sentencers

A total of 372 questionnaires were sent to Leeds magistrates in November 1990 and 193 replies were received (a response rate of 52 per cent); of the 193, 109 (56 per cent) stated that they had heard of the Leeds IP scheme, although three of these said 'only vaguely' and did not answer any other questions (two of the 84 who had not heard of it asked why they had not). Table 5.12 sets out what Leeds magistrates understood the aims of the local IP scheme to be.

The three most common responses were the same as those given by the Durham magistrates, with the most popular by far being that IP aimed to offer an alternative to custody; to tackle offending behaviour was mentioned quite often here but hardly at all at Durham, but this may reflect the fact that the Leeds IP scheme had been running for several years while that at Durham had just got underway.

Once again, social work tasks are seen as the main components of the IP programme with more control-oriented responses taking a back seat. The views of magistrates on the kinds of offences for which IP might be used and the offenders who might be 'sentenced' to IP are listed in Tables 5.14 and 5.15. Although there may appear to be some confusion about the age-range for IP amongst Leeds magistrates, this is more likely to reflect the fact that there are two separate schemes in the city, one of which caters for 17-20 year olds while the other focuses on those over 21.

Table 5.12
Aims of the Leeds IP project

Aim	Number of mentions
Alternative to/Reduce the use of custody	65
Reduce offending	35
More intensive supervision	21
Tackle offending behaviour	18
Rehabilitation of offenders	17
Treatment geared to the needs of the individual	17
Last chance when other options have failed	3
Other (keep to a contract between officer and offender, don't know)	2

Table 5.13 sets out what magistrates said they expected the IP programme to offer.

Table 5.13
What offenders might do on an IP scheme

Activity	Number of mentions
Examine offending behaviour	51
Comply with requirements/Co-operate	24
Participate in a planned, individualised programme	19
Learn a more structured life-style	15
Keep in regular contact with probation officers	15
Tackle individual problems	12
Learn to take responsibility	11
Learn social/vocational/leisure skills	11
Learn from their mistakes	7
Group work	5
Other (inc. community work, one-to-one work, meet victims, "avoid the requirements as far as possible")	8

Table 5.14
Offences for which IP might be used

Offence	Number of mentions
Theft	45
Burglary	39
Alternative to custody	32
Car theft	26
Violence	12
Serious offences	11
Drug/Alcohol related	9
Public order	7
Criminal damage	6
Deception	6
Motoring	5
Failures on other community disposals	5
Other (inc. not violence, not sexual, offender more important than offence, any)	17

Table 5.15
Offenders who might be placed on IP

Offender	Number of mentions
Those at risk of custody	36
Those who are willing to change	30
Persistent offenders	28
Those who have failed on probation/CSO	15
Young offenders	11
17-20 year olds	10
Those over 21	10
Those with alcohol/drug problems	8
Those with a poor family background	8
Any for whom it is considered suitable	8
Other (inc. non-violent, few previous convictions, stable background)	10

As the Leeds schemes had been running for some time before the questionnaire was circulated to magistrates, it is not surprising that of the 106 respondents who completed the questionnaire, 42 (40 per cent) said that they had visited the IP scheme.

Table 5.16 shows how respondents saw IP fitting into the range of disposals which were available.

Table 5.16
"How do you see IP fitting into the range of sentencing options available?"

Position	Number of mentions
Alternative to custody	25
Another useful option	22
"Very well"	10
More useful for Crown Court	5
Depends on results	4
For those who have rehabilitative potential	3
Between probation and community service	3
Other (inc. alternative to CSO/custody, same level as CSO, after probation/CSO, between probation and custody)	17

As was the case with Durham, it is possible to see a certain tension in the view of IP as an alternative to custody and as another useful option. The advantages and disadvantages of IP as seen by the Leeds magistrates are set out in Tables 5.17 and 5.18.

Table 5.17
Advantages of IP

Advantage	Number of mentions
Diversion from/Reduce the use of custody	28
Reduce offending	22
Could reform/rehabilitate	18
Offers help/support for offenders	15
Challenges old habits	15
Gives offenders the chance to start again	12
Focus on the individual	10
Tackles offending behaviour	8
Cost effective	7
Keeps offenders in the community	5
Other (inc. brings structure to offenders' lives, another option, more demanding than custody, none)	10

Table 5.18
Disadvantages of IP

Disadvantage	Number of mentions
Offenders may see it as a soft option	36
Public may see it as a soft option	24
None	11
Must be run to the strictest standards	10
Risk of further offending as community-based	9
Under-resourced	7
Not enough time on the scheme	5
Very dedicated staff needed	4
Expensive	4
Offenders may prove unwilling to change	4
Other (inc. post-IP adjustment, assessment difficulties, failure lead to harsh sentence, no punishment element)	23

The advantages are heavily weighted towards the helping aspects of IP; as with Durham, the major drawback is that IP may be seen as a soft option. Other comments on the Leeds IP scheme were supportive, although it was noted that the scheme was very reliant on the probation officers' recommendation. The need for adequate funding and for IP to be run strictly were also mentioned often. One magistrate thought that IP was needed in all probation orders and used the slogan 'LISP for all'.

Four judges who sat in Leeds Crown Court and were therefore expected to have had some knowledge and/or experience of IP were also interviewed; they were very much in favour of intensive probation. They were aware of the two schemes, and one judge had visited them and another had arranged a visit. The information provided about the Leeds IP schemes was considered to be very helpful and informative. Essentially, they saw IP as being for serious, persistent offenders who were at risk of custody although offences such as rape and murder were not seen as applicable. The advantages of IP were seen as lying in its individualised programme and the fact that more time and effort could be spent in trying to help offenders with their problems. Few disadvantages were mentioned; the financial costs might be high and the public – and particularly victims – might see IP as a soft option. IP was considered to be an alternative to a custodial sentence, and on the whole was expected to reduce offending more effectively than other sentences.

The views of probation officers

This section reports the views of probation officers, including those who had referred to the Edge or LISP and those who had not done so. Fifteen officers were selected for interview as follows: the eight SPOs heading the field teams were consulted and four agreed to nominate their officers; the ACPO chairing the meeting agreed that this would present a range of opinions about IP. On visiting each field team, all officers who happened to be available were interviewed. Two of the teams operated from offices in the suburbs while the other two operated from the office in the town centre which also housed the LISP team.

Hardly any of the maingrade officers had made more than five or six referrals over the last two years, and not all of these had been accepted by the project or made into IP orders by the court, so that individual officers tended to have little experience of actually supervising offenders on IP. Despite this lack of contact, most were aware of IP and of the two projects in Leeds. One or two of the probation officers who had used IP commented that they were happy that there was someone else who could spend so much time with the probationer since they did not have the time to carry out such intensive supervision. In practice, they had found both the LISP workers and the Edge workers easy to liaise with. Others were not convinced that it would be useful in preventing reoffending or solving problems but were happy to recommend it if they thought it might be more likely to keep people out of prison.

A few who had not used IP argued there was no need for intensive supervision since they regarded a straight probation order or an order with a requirement as being intensive enough to provide an alternative to custody which would adequately address the offender's needs. It was considered that these probationers, although at risk of custody, did not actually need intensive supervision. There was also concern that, although attractive to the courts, IP would raise an individual up tariff unnecessarily. Where there was a need for more intensive supervision, those officers felt able to provide the same package themselves with the help of Probation Service Assistants and volunteers. This way, the offender was offered intensive supervision in the form of more frequent regular contact than a normal straight probation order, but it would still be called a straight probation order.

In addition to this, IP was opposed in principle by these officers as they considered that its presentation as a high tariff community sentence downgraded the status of a straight probation order, leaving maingrade officers feeling that they were only expected to work with less serious offenders. This had had a somewhat demoralising effect on some staff who felt they had been trained to supervise all kinds of offenders in the community but that these skills were being wasted as the more 'interesting' cases were farmed out.

Alongside the issue of de-skilling was the complaint that some probation officers felt they could carry out intensive supervision with offenders themselves if they had the resources that were currently being allocated to the IP projects. There was some consistency across field teams in their resentment of an apparent lack of resources allocated to projects being run by individual offices (such as alcohol education groups) and it was this diversion of resources from the work of maingrade officers to the work of what was seen to be an 'elite' group which lay at the heart of much of the frustration with IP. However, this frustration seemed to be directed more towards LISP than the Edge, since the Edge was not wholly funded by West Yorkshire Probation Service.

Not all non-referring probation officers opposed IP in principle. There were a few who had not used IP at all simply because they felt they had not had anybody who would have been 'suitable' for it, although they would have referred them if they had.

Where officers had referred to one project more often than the other, this was either because they tended to be allocated individuals of a particular age, thus falling into the age bracket of one or the other project, or, for one or two officers, because they preferred the ethos of one project to the other.

The main objection to LISP stemmed from its past incarnation as 'tracking' and the project had found it very difficult to shake off this image. In addition to this, some probation officers preferred the philosophy and the methods of the Edge because it was set up in full consultation with NAPO so that probation officers were able to voice their concerns and exert some influence on the eventual shape of the programme. While LISP was later modified in the light of similar (but belated) consultation, service managers appeared to have learnt from experience the importance not only of consulting widely, but of making sure this happened at the beginning of the project rather than half way through in response to some difficulty. Basically, this meant working proactively rather than reactively in order to avoid later difficulties with implementation.

Despite eventual consultation, some probation officers continued to object to fundamental aspects of the LISP programme which were not altered. One was the additional level of management in the project whereby maingrade probation officers were given a management role in the day to day supervision of programme workers. To some extent this meant that the supervising officers felt they were no longer 'driving' the order in that a LISP probation officer was involved in making decisions about breach situations; however, this concern operated also on a personal level since one of the probation liaison officers had particularly strong views on how the project should be run. It was felt that the responsibility of the maingrade officer had been compromised by the LISP management structure. At the same time, the probation liaison officers were seen as having too much autonomy while, simultaneously, maingrade officers were expected to become more accountable. Supervising officers often felt that when they made a referral, LISP tended to wrest control of the order from the supervising officer.

In practice, some elements of the LISP programme which met with disapproval were the use of conditional bail assessment when people were already on bail, the perceived inflexibility of 60 days of contact for all offenders irrespective of their actual needs, and what was perceived as the overly punitive aspect of the programme in its focus on offending behaviour when other problems may have been more pressing. In addition, where the Edge had occasionally been criticised for not placing enough emphasis on protecting the public, LISP had been criticised for occasionally putting too much emphasis on this aspect of their work and not focusing enough on the offender's needs. For example, one probation officer reported that one person she had referred to LISP had been wrongly breached and had successfully appealed against it.

Several probation officers felt more comfortable referring people to LISP than to the Edge because the former was run by the probation service; this reflected trust of an organisation which shared the same professional philosophy, and distrust of a project which took more of a social work approach. However, it was surprising, given initial concerns, that there was very little criticism of the practical aspects of working in partnership with a voluntary body. In practice, the familiarity of the probation liaison officers with the court system was thought to contrast sharply with the Edge project workers' lack of experience in this area: a couple of probation officers (in different offices) cited project workers' practice of referring to offenders in court by their first name. (These presentations had been dubbed 'Little Johnny' reports by some sentencers.)

Some officers were also wary of the Edge's commitment to the concept of 'public safety' and had little confidence that the Edge was recording all instances of offending while on the programme. Another aspect which reinforced the idea that LISP was notionally closer to the probation service was the fact that it was located in the same building as three of the field teams. This proximity appeared significantly to increase confidence in the project and facilitate liaison. Overall, then, there were very few criticisms of the Edge compared to LISP, but probation officers seemed to trust LISP more because it was a probation run project.

The views of managers

This section reports how managers and those involved in the setting up of IP thought it had gone in the light of the original aims of the projects. Semi-structured interviews were carried out with the West Yorkshire DCPO, the ACPO for the Leeds specialist teams, the Replacements to Custody SPO, the two probation liaison officers at LISP and the manager of the Edge.

The main aims of both LISP and the Edge had been to divert offenders from custody and to prevent offenders from reoffending, both for the duration of the IP order and in the longer term. After two years of running both programmes, managers at West Yorkshire were content that the first of these aims had been met in the light of their monitoring data and the evaluation study being carried out at Leeds University. These showed high Risk of Custody scores, considerable previous experience of custody and that the most common disposal for referrals who were not given IP was custody (as described above). It was considered that, in the short term, the programmes had successfully prevented offenders from reoffending given that a high proportion completed the programme without prosecution for further offences, and that those who did reoffend did so less seriously and less frequently than before. Managers were waiting for more people to finish their probation order before they could say whether reoffending had been reduced in the longer term.

In retrospect, the experience of IP was seen to have been fraught with difficulties, and this was especially true for LISP although most of the problems appeared to have been cleared up before IP monitoring began. One of the main problems with LISP at this time was that its development had been a bottom-up process and was consequently not planned or managed as well as it might have been. The fact that LISP developed from a programme which had aroused some controversy ('tracking') gave rise to a number of problems in getting the programme accepted by maingrade officers. Despite eventual consultation with NAPO, there remained a sense of disquiet among referring officers. However, LISP was under way when monitoring began and many of the teething problems that might be expected in the development of any project had largely been sorted out.

The same was true of the Edge project in that it had been running for a year before monitoring began. Before then, development of the Edge project had been very different to that of LISP, given that it started from scratch and involved partnership with a voluntary body. This factor was controversial in that several people were uncomfortable with the idea of a voluntary body carrying out probation work. However, senior probation managers felt that it was managed better than LISP in terms of its implementation and as a result it got off to a good start. In fact, it took more referrals than anticipated and quickly became oversubscribed. Consequently, LISP expanded its age range and took several referrals from the Edge who were under 21. The Edge project, then, had had fewer problems than LISP in its early stages of development, but after its first year changes had been made and its mode of practice was fairly well established.

Once both projects were up and running, managers felt that the quality of work of both was of a high standard. In addition to the benefits afforded by the projects in terms of diversions from custody and the positive experiences for offenders, it was thought that the IP experience had resulted in positive outcomes for the service. Both projects had challenged the organisational culture and traditional methods of working within the service by allocating serious offenders to specific projects rather than including them in the normal caseloads. These new methods of working were significantly different from the usual supervision practice in that they involved frequent contact alongside work on offending behaviour and offenders' needs, balancing this with the protection of the public. Both projects attracted additional resources to the division and the service was able to exploit the voluntary sector's experience in public relations and resource acquisition. As a result of this and the actual programmes, it was felt that IP had significantly raised the credibility of the service with sentencers.

Alongside the benefits, there remained a few problems with IP. One of these was that because the projects only dealt with high tariff offenders, they were seen as elitist: this was especially true at LISP where the programme workers were being managed on a day to day basis by maingrade probation officers. Senior managers felt that it might have been better if the liaison posts were held by senior probation officers in future. Both projects were thought to have failed to provide equity of access to field teams across the division, and to black and female offenders in particular. Both projects were equipped to deal with female and black offenders, but few referrals were made by field teams. One problem specific to the Edge was the insecurity of the project in view of the fact that it was only being funded in the short term. This was especially inconvenient given the amount of time and resources that had been required at the beginning to set up the partnership, which it was felt had not been adequately anticipated. A problem experienced by both projects, according to senior managers, concerned the transfer of offenders from the IP order to the probation order at the end where it was felt that there was not enough preparation at present.

Managers were asked how they saw IP fitting in with the new Criminal Justice Act. The Act was expected to have little impact on the implementation of IP, other than a possible increase in referrals, since they felt they were already operating in the spirit of the Act. Following the Act, intensive supervision would become known as 'Intensive Probation' and would be a legal addition to a supervision order.

In the future, IP was set to become available across the whole of West Yorkshire; there were a couple of other IP projects already running but they had evolved separately from the Leeds initiatives. However, there was a marked preference for including IP in the form of LISP rather than the NCH partnership which was being retained as long as it brought in additional resources. Of the two in Leeds, LISP was viewed as the definitive model of intensive supervision. Thus, existing projects would be encouraged to convert to the LISP model in an attempt to standardise service provision across the division.

The views of offenders

Semi-structured interviews were carried out with ten offenders in West Yorkshire, half of whom were on the Edge programme and the other half on LISP. It was hoped that many more would be interviewed, but in practice it was very difficult to find and get hold of offenders to interview them. Of the ten interviewed, three had already finished the programme once and were now on it for the second time. Of the rest, two had just finished, one was due to finish in 1 week, three in 2 weeks and one in 3 weeks. All of them had expected to go to prison for periods ranging between 3 months and 5 years, and were generally pleased when they heard they had been sentenced to intensive probation instead of custody, although they had not known what it was.

Those participating in IP at LISP found the first weeks more difficult than those at the Edge since the high frequency of contact was felt to be quite intrusive; however, this was later thought to be worth it as they gradually formed a relationship with their programme worker who became more like a 'friend' who they could talk to and who could help sort out their problems.

At both projects, the offenders spent much time talking about their offending and why they did it, and on a more practical level, about problems such as accommodation and finding a job. The fact that there was always someone to discuss these matters and help sort out problems was highly valued, especially when compared to the fact that both at home and in prison there was usually no-one they could discuss such things with. As one offender said, "It gives you a chance to look at what you're doing: in prison you didn't get a chance to talk about things and you come out the same as when you went in." Most thought the programme should be longer, especially those at the Edge who, even though they were about to finish their order, intended to keep coming back to "chat about problems." Several on both programmes thought that it should be of longer duration in order to help with more long-term problems such as drug or alcohol misuse, but there did not appear to be any problems of disengagement from the programme/project worker at the end of the order (although this would be more likely to become apparent later on). For those still on IP, contact was much less frequent than it had been at the beginning and they felt that if they had any problems afterwards they could approach their supervising probation officer.

All the offenders felt that the experience had been worthwhile, not only in that it had kept them out of prison, but because it had kept them out of trouble and prevented them from reoffending. Time spent on the LISP programme had helped them think more carefully about what they were going to do during the day, and the younger group at the Edge had especially valued being able to talk to people about their offending and associated problems. In summation, the view of those who had completed LISP was that it had been hard but it was worth it; those at the Edge thought that it had been enjoyable and extremely useful.

Summary

When LISP and the Edge were originally set up, the projects aimed to provide alternatives to custody for serious offenders within two different age ranges: 17-20 and 21 and over. In practice, the majority of referrals were within the required age range for each project. The development of the projects differed significantly in that one, LISP, had already been running as a high-tariff community penalty when it was adapted for IP, whereas the other was started from scratch. Both had teething problems, for example, in getting probation officers to accept that the actual work with offenders was not going to be carried out by maingrade officers but by probation service assistants (LISP) and social work professionals (the Edge). Interestingly, however, it was the project which had already been running (LISP) which seemed to encounter the more serious problems with gaining acceptance by NAPO. This appeared to be largely due to existing problems and a seeming lack of negotiation about the design of the project, unlike the Edge which engaged in negotiations right at the beginning. Although many probation officers had originally felt uncomfortable with the idea of working with a voluntary organisation, in the case of the Edge, this turned out not to be a problem at all, although maingrade officers remained sceptical about the extent to which the Edge paid attention to the issue of public protection.

Although it was not possible to say whether those actually sentenced to IP would otherwise have definitely received custodial sentences, it was nonetheless possible to assess the accuracy of the projects' targeting in terms of the seriousness of offenders referred. Referrals to both projects appeared to be at risk of custody in that they had serious offending histories (evidenced by serious previous offences and previous custody) and serious current offences, along with a high risk of custody score which, of course, summarised this information.

Furthermore, analysis of those referrals who were actually sentenced to IP showed them to be closer on a number of seriousness measures to those sentenced to custody than to a comparison group of offenders sentenced to community service. In all, this suggests that IP was indeed being used as an alternative to custody.

Those involved in the setting up of IP were generally pleased with the way in which it had developed and was working. Despite the fact that both projects appeared successful, probation managers were generally in agreement that LISP would continue and provide a model for future IP projects in the division, whilst the Edge, although it was in itself considered successful, would only continue as long as the probation service did not have to fund it completely. Offenders gave the impression that, while IP had helped them considerably in sorting out practical problems, it needed to go on for longer if it was to have a more substantial effect on offending behaviour.

Finally, although there was not a great response from sentencers, those who had heard of IP gave the impression that they agreed with its aims and saw it as an important alternative to custody, especially in that it provided a significant level of social work input while at the same time reducing offending.

6 Intensive Probation in the West Midlands

Introduction

Intensive probation (IP) in the West Midlands was qualitatively very different from the schemes run in either Leeds or Durham. In the first place, it had been applied to four large divisions in the West of the county: Wolverhampton, Walsall, Sandwell and Dudley, all of which had previously operated in relative independence. As a result, IP covered a much greater catchment area than the other two projects. As an indicator, these divisions had more than 700 magistrates, in comparison with Leeds which had fewer than 400. Secondly, and most significantly, IP in the West Midlands was never set up as a new scheme offering a different approach to supervising young offenders. The aim of senior management was rather to achieve standardisation across probation teams and divisions; and to focus attention on the target group of young offenders at risk of custody. There were no 'centres' or 'schemes' of IP; it was the responsibility of all field probation officers to integrate it into their daily workload. These factors resulted in a far more diffuse feeling to the initiative and for this and other reasons which will be looked at in detail below, it proved more difficult to research.

As was the case with Leeds and Durham, the West Midlands had been suffering from a high rate of young adult incarceration in the late 1980s and was therefore seen as an appropriate area for the introduction of an IP scheme by the Home Office, in line with the Green Paper and the Tackling Offending Initiative. In the spring of 1989, the senior management of West Midlands Probation Service (WMPS) laid out its plans for the introduction of intensive probation in response to the letter sent to CPOs in February. At this stage it was made clear that, while intensive probation would be a "distinctive new initiative", it would essentially involve an extension of the intensive supervision already offered at day centres in the county. It was felt that 4A and 4B programmes already fitted the Home Office description of intensive probation and to introduce an additional, higher tariff order would have undermined them. Wolverhampton and Walsall were targeted as areas without their own day centres and therefore eligible for IP. Despite having their own day centres, Sandwell and Dudley were also included on the basis that all four divisions shared the same Crown Court at Wolverhampton. At that point, it was envisaged that IP would focus primarily on the Crown Court. Coventry was considered too small, and Birmingham, though central, was thought to have adequate day centre provision.

A major motivation for the introduction of IP was therefore standardisation. Day centre provision was not uniform across the county: while divisions that did not have day centres could use those of neighbouring divisions, this was often impractical if offenders needed to travel long distances. What senior management really wanted was new day centres in Wolverhampton and Walsall. However, while capital was awaited for this purpose, it was thought that IP would provide a "stop-gap", ensuring that intensive supervision would be available throughout the county. It was also hoped that IP could be used as a means of ensuring the universal acceptance and use of Cambridgeshire Risk of Custody scale. Prior to the introduction of IP, various ROC scales were used in some teams and none in others. By defining the target group for IP on the basis of CROC scores, senior management aimed to ensure global usage of the CROC scale. Lastly, a further motivation for IP's introduction was the hope of future resources. While no probation services received direct, central funding for setting up IP schemes, the letter from the Home Office stated that it "would give priority to areas which operate IP programmes when allocating funds for capital expenditure on day centres, CS workshops, probation offices and probation hostels." By showing commitment to IP, senior management hoped to receive financial resources in the future. The West Midlands probation aims for IP, therefore, were not in line with those of the Home Office.

Objectives

Despite the fact that IP was to be introduced in four divisions, each with an ACPO, the major responsibility for the development of IP was given to one of these ACPOs. An SPO was also employed to work on the introduction of IP, part of whose brief was to draw up an IP practice manual. At the beginning of 1990 a steering committee was set up including an SPO from each division. Later that year the practice manual for staff was produced, detailing objectives for targeting, SIR preparation and supervision of IPs.

In line with the original response to the CPO letter, the steering committee recognised that demanding alternatives to custody already existed in all four divisions. As a result, the steering committee decided that, rather than try to identify an even more serious stratum of offenders to divert from custody, IP orders would simply become the sole high tariff probation order for 17 to 20 year olds. Further, divisions would be encouraged to share resources (such as day centres, sports and employment facilities) whenever appropriate, in order to facilitate an increasingly interactive and homogenous service across the divisions. The work manual spelled out in more detail how IP would be targeted. While IP would be the sole probation order available for high tariff young adult offenders, CSOs would also be available for this target group, but would be reserved for offenders requiring less social work input. Young adults appearing at the Crown Court with a CROC score of 60 or over should be considered for assessment. However, the manual stressed that professional judgement should also be utilised and could take precedence over CROC scores. This was especially relevant at the magistrates court, where a significant number of custodial sentences had been given to young adults with CROC scores as low as 25.

The manual included quite detailed plans for presenting IP packages to the court. SIRs recommending IP were to be more offence-focused: social background information needed to be related to defendants' offending behaviour. They were also to be shorter, due to the introduction of a 'Personal Action Plan' and a 'Programme Content', which were to accompany the SIR and which would cover some of the ground usually included in a regular SIR. The personal action plan was to set out generalised goals and targets for improving behaviour. The programme content was to provide specific information on how these goals were to be realised. On the subject of programme content, the manual was quite clear that "IP should be characterised by the inclusion of an additional condition/s as originally suggested by the Home Office". In nearly all cases this was to include specified Schedule 11 requirements and where appropriate, components supervised by voluntary sector organisations. In the case of the latter, a report could be prepared by the relevant voluntary body and included in the programme content section. Special forms were developed for the personal action plan and programme content. Agreement forms were also specially produced for offenders to sign.

The involvement of voluntary organisations was an important part of the IP initiative. Two voluntary bodies were targeted particularly for co-working on IP. The first of these, the Rainer Foundation received Home Office funding for working with offenders on IP. There were two offices in the target area - one in Wolverhampton and one in Dudley, each staffed by a project manager and project worker and each receiving a grant of £50,000. It was envisaged that Rainer would provide an accommodation and employment service to offenders on IP. The second voluntary body, the ARK Foundation in Wolverhampton, consisted of a well-equipped gymnasium in the basement of a Methodist church. The aim of the couple who ran it and the ethos of the Foundation in general, was to reduce alcohol abuse and violent behaviour in the young, with an emphasis on demanding physical training. The ARK foundation received £50,000 funding from the probation service. Although work with voluntary bodies was to be included as separate components in the programme content, the staff manual clearly stated that this work constituted voluntary components of IP.

With regard to intensity of contact, the staff manual clearly stated that 'IPs will demand a higher level of contact than ordinary Probation Orders'. While not prescribing a precise level of intensity for the first six months of the order, the manual stressed that the minimum level of contact should be one per week with the probation service. However, there is no comparison made with supervision of 4A/4B orders, and therefore no indication that IP would involve any more intensity of contact than the orders it was to replace.

Finally, IP breach practice was defined by the staff manual as follows: "More than three unacceptable absences will result in enforcement proceedings".

IP orders therefore were supposed to differ from the old 4A/4B orders in a number of respects. Perhaps most important was the new name, the significance of which should not be underestimated. However much sentencers and field teams were told that IP orders were broadly similar to what had gone before, many in both groups were expecting something radically different. Unfortunately this dilemma was never fully resolved over the period that intensive probation was available. Nevertheless, there were other differences. Voluntary bodies had been funded by the Home Office to contribute to the supervision of offenders on IP, and probation officers were expected to make more use of these resources. SIR preparation was to be more standardised: reports were to be shorter, more offence-focused and accompanied by special attachments detailing the objectives and content of the order. Special IP paperwork was produced for this purpose. Another distinctive feature was that IP orders were to involve multiple components. Of course, 4A and 4B orders already consisted of at least two components: offenders had to participate in at least one specified activity or attend a day centre and must also receive regular supervision from their probation officer. However, the implication of the staff manual was that IP orders would involve more parts - the extra component presumably being the voluntary sector work. IP orders were also to be subject to a simple and standardised breach practice. A more cynical view of IP however in this area would be of 'old wine in new bottles'.

Implementation

The introduction of IP into the West Midlands in September 1990 was not readily received from SPO level down. Despite consistent attempts to clarify its use as outlined above by the ACPO in charge, there was a great deal of confusion about how and when IP should be recommended and SPOs from different divisions gave conflicting instructions to their staff regarding these matters. There was also active resistance from some field teams who felt that IP had been a top down imposition with no consultation at their level regarding practice and policy (this decreased over time but by no means disappeared).

NAPO representatives expressed concern about various issues: that the service had been undermined by the granting of money to voluntary bodies whose workers did not necessarily have professional training; and about the possibility of net widening, the degree of control involved in the new initiative and how this might set up the young offenders to fail, resulting in custody. This was in spite of top management's decision to reject the option of what they called a 'tracking' scheme as it was too punitive and consequently at variance with the ethos of the WMPS.

The result of this confusion and resistance was a low rate of referral for IP orders; and where orders were made there was considerable variety in practice. In the first ten months that IP was an option in the West Midlands, there were only 86 recommendations for it, of which 65 orders were made.

This number was much lower than senior management had expected for what was supposed to be the sole high tariff probation alternative to custody in the area, and management became aware that many young offenders were still receiving 4A and 4B recommendations in their SIRs. As a gatekeeping strategy, they stipulated that as of

January 1991, in all four IP divisions, every 17-20 year old for whom an SIR was being prepared had to have a RPU IP monitoring form filled out for them in order to get some measure of the proportion slipping through the net. However, rather than having the desired effect, this instruction further annoyed many officers who were already irritated by the amount of new paperwork involved in making SIR applications for IP, and referrals did not seem to increase significantly.

Towards the end of the IP initiative, senior management decided to dispense with the special IP paperwork, in the hope that this would lead to more IP recommendations. While this may have led to an increase in recommendations, the loss of the paperwork meant further confusion as to what constituted an IP order. IP became indistinguishable from probation with a 4A or 4B condition. Finally, senior management announced that IP was to end at the end of March 1992.

What IP entailed in the West Midlands

Despite the efforts of the ACPO and SPO co-ordinating the introduction of IP, there were great variations in practice between divisions, teams and individual officers, depending on the degree of resistance to IP and the extent of knowledge of recommended IP practice.

Staffing

As already noted, an SPO was appointed to devise the work manual. When this had been completed, he moved elsewhere and another SPO was appointed – a Crown Court Liaison Officer who oversaw the dissemination and collection of the RPU IP monitoring forms for the four divisions. Other than this position, there were no appointments specifically linked to the introduction of IP: referral and supervision of the participants were carried out directly by field probation officers. At the start, one or two field officers in each team were asked to liaise with other staff on any recommendations for IP going forward to the court as an extra check on tariff rating and paperwork. Although this continued to happen informally in some teams, it was largely dropped principally because of staffing changes but also because of the low number of referrals.

The referral process

According to the manual, any young offender (17-20) with a Cambridgeshire Risk of Custody (CROC) score of 60 or over at Crown Court or 25 or over at magistrates' court was to be considered for IP. This was determined by assessing the threshold risk of custody score at which sentencers had been known to send offenders to custody in the past. However, it was stressed that the CROC score should only be used as a trigger, not as a determinant.

While the manual guidelines seemed fairly clear, on the ground confusion reigned. The magistrates' court CROC threshold of 25 caused particular bafflement. In many teams, it was assumed that this was a prescriptive threshold for IP: if an offender appeared at a magistrates court with a CROC score of 25 or over, they must be recommended for an IP order or a CSO. This conclusion stemmed from the fact that IP had been described as the sole high-tariff probation order. The chain of logic ran that if offenders with a CROC score of 25 were at risk of custody, they must be high tariff and therefore must be eligible for an IP order. In fact, this was a fallacy. The manual had made it clear that CROC scores were only a guideline: professional judgement should also be utilised, and this was particularly true of the magistrates' court. However, the message had not got through.

The result was that, rather than recommend IP for all offenders with CROC scores over 25 at the magistrates' courts, various local practices developed. In one team, the 25 CROC limit was ignored, and the limit adopted at both courts was 65. One probation officer in another team had adopted a level of 75 at either court, another in the same team was working on the basis of 60 at either court. In another team, the limit at both courts was set at 25. Not surprisingly, there was considerable concern expressed in this team about the possibility of net-widening. Nearly every probation officer and SPO interviewed expressed the view that the CROC score targeting at the magistrates' court had been highly damaging to the credibility of IP amongst field teams: in the words of one officer it had been "a fiasco".

A further problem for the IP referral process was that, as described above, 4A and 4B orders were still being made for young offenders. In some cases these orders continued to be used instead of IP orders for the IP target group, because individual officers either refused to recommend the new order, or did not understand the practice guidelines. However, in other cases 4A orders were being used for low tariff offenders. Contrary to the senior management view, a number of SPOs and probation officers stated that 4A orders had often been used as a low tariff probation order prior to the introduction of IP. It was therefore felt that they should continue to be used in this way. The example was given of a low tariff offender who had a serious alcohol problem and could not be expected to attend an alcohol group voluntarily. In such cases a 4A order could be made with a condition that he/she should attend the group. This practice continued in a number of teams.

Where IP referrals were made, one or two lengthy assessment interviews were conducted by the field team probation officer. As was the case with other areas, these interviews could take place in prison if the candidate was on remand. Similarly, the officer's task was to identify the individual's particular problems, attempt to assess his/her motivation to change through perception of the offence and response to previous sentences, and look at ways in which problems could be addressed if the recommendation was successful at court. If the officer was convinced at the end of the assessment that the person was appropriate for IP, a recommendation would be made to the court.

Work done while on IP

Before embarking on a description of the nature of work done on IP, it should be noted that, because of resource constraints the bulk of observational research was carried out in the Wolverhampton and Walsall divisions, although some work was also done in Sandwell and Dudley. Further, the observational work carried out in these areas was limited in comparison to Leeds and Durham as POs were unwilling for researchers to observe IP group work 'in vivo' for fear of it affecting the group work itself.

The content of the programmes run in the West Midlands differed considerably from those in Leeds and Durham, essentially in terms of amount of contact with the participant. It was stressed in the work manual that for the first six months, minimum contact was once a week; the number of contacts as well as the nature of these and the demands they made on the offender were to be spelled out for the sentencer and participant in the programme content document. Because of opposition to the notion of enforced contact with offenders amongst a substantial proportion of maingrade officers, the large number of those who had offenders on IP kept contact to a bare minimum in the first six months (it should be added that the key issue was whether this was spelt out to the court and was being adhered to). Some officers chose to ignore this stipulation and continued to see their participants at fortnightly intervals as it was felt that more frequent contact would not be of any use to the offender, although where a participant was required to attend a day centre three days a week as a condition of IP, and meet with their PO once a week, contact approached the intensity of other probation services. However, in many cases, where, for instance, day centres were not available, IP consisted of attendance at a group once a week, plus one contact with the PO.

The work that was done with participants was of a high quality. A wide range of group work was on offer, and there was some evidence of sending participants to groups in other divisions if this was necessary and viable. Groups included offending behaviour, alcohol education, motoring offending, finance and budgeting, sex offending and women's issues. Groups ran for up to 11 weeks (though most were six) and usually lasted up to two hours per session. Of particular interest was the offending behaviour group run at Walsall. This was a six week course run by two officers with extensive experience of running groups. About half way into the course, the participants would make a video of an offence that one member had recently committed. The following weeks were spent replaying parts of the video and looking at points in the decision making process where the offender could make the choice not to commit the crime. The group would finally make an alternative video, portraying a scenario which the group created itself, in which the participants chose not to commit the crime in question.

Liaison with voluntary bodies proved problematic. There was no history of close co-working between WMPS and the voluntary sector before the advent of IP. What experience there had been had consisted of local team-based initiatives. The new emphasis on co-operation strengthened what was already a considerable distrust of voluntary bodies among many probation officers. Where this attitude held sway, there was little hope of Rainer or ARK making an impression. Thus, one of the Rainer staff described how even within the same division, some teams had shown considerable interest in working with them, while others were completely unapproachable. There was also the problem that where probation officers did have pre-IP links with a voluntary body, these channels tended to go on being used for IP. Over the study period, funding for the APEX trust, which was used by a number of teams for employment training, was greatly reduced. It was hoped that teams would then turn to Rainer.

Where Rainer or ARK were used, the reaction of officers was usually positive. One officer described the "excellent work" done by Rainer staff: he cited their ability to follow up offenders even when they were imprisoned, visiting them inside and then making contact with them on their release. There were also negative comments – one officer stated that Rainer had "let clients down"; another that they had "not come up with the goods". A more explicit criticism was that Rainer had originally been funded to provide employment training and help with accommodation. They had failed to provide any help with the latter. The most frequently mentioned positive comment was that the involvement of Rainer and ARK in IP had led to much greater awareness of what the voluntary sector had to offer. Thus, even if Rainer and ARK were not used to the full over IP, the conceptual jump had been made for some officers: they were prepared to look outside the service for agencies to take on certain aspects of work on an order. It should be noted that the special IP SIR paperwork which included a section on voluntary agencies may have contributed to this process. One probation officer stated that the SIR format had led to the consideration of voluntary agencies becoming part of formalised practice.

A recurrent issue affecting voluntary sector participation was that some officers were unsure whether offenders could be breached for non-attendance at a voluntary agency scheme. The staff manual made it clear that this was not the case – and this was reiterated by the ACPO responsible for IP, but the myth seemed to survive. While the majority of officers were clear that all such attendance was voluntary, some did point out that if offenders were brought to court in breach of another (probation-supervised) component of their order, non-attendance on voluntary work could be included in evidence.

The ARK foundation had its own local problems in that its social work ethos was somewhat at variance with that of the probation service. The latter preferred that the ARK did not attempt to do social work at all, but rather engaged the participant's time in as fruitful a pursuit as possible – i.e. athletic training towards a particular goal. The director was a passionate exponent of the foundation's motto and aim: 'Through abstinence and guidance we will overcome', and unfortunately, this was not well received by field teams. Several POs reported reluctance to refer there.

The Rainer foundation, for most of the first ten months that IP was available, was understaffed. This, coupled with probation officers' hesitation to utilise the service for all the reasons mentioned above, caused problems regarding the number of referrals. Those that worked in the organisation were well motivated and offered a useful service, aiming to see the participant about twice a week during the programme and attempting to have them placed in employment or employment training by the end of the programme. A substantial amount of time was spent on social and interview skills and those supervising the participants for this element of the programme had more time at their disposal for support and follow-up. The few POs who used this service were impressed at both the quality of input with participants and report writing. Rainer staff were disappointed, however, at what they saw as a low level of referrals. Extra staff were recruited during the second half of the monitoring period and the service was relaunched.

Findings from the monitoring

Referrals for IP were monitored over 17 months, between the starting date (September 1990) and the end of March 1992 when IP officially ended in the West Midlands. Over this period, 187 people in the West Midlands were considered for IP. This figure includes those who were recommended for IP in their SIR or who were referred for assessment for IP or who were sentenced to IP by the courts.

Demographic information

Almost all referrals were male (96 per cent). Ages ranged between 17 and 21 with a mean of 19 years. All therefore fell within the intended age limits of the IP initiative.

The ethnic group of most referrals was categorised as white (84 per cent); 16 per cent were non-white, described variously as Black-Caribbean (seven per cent), Black-Other (two per cent), Indian (three per cent), Chinese (one per cent) and Other (four per cent). The great majority of referrals were unemployed (78 per cent), with only 15 per cent working and three per cent on government training schemes (four per cent were unavailable for work).

Seriousness of referrals

Table 6.1 shows the Risk of Custody scores of the referrals and, as can be seen, only 52 per cent scored more than 70. The mean Risk of Custody score was 69 per cent.

Table 6.1
Risk of Custody scores for all referrals

Score (%)	n	%
0-50	48	(29)
51-70	30	(19)
71-99	57	(35)
100[1]	28	(17)
Total[2]	163	(100)

1 One case scored 125 on the CROC scale
2 Information was unavailable for 24 referrals

Fewer than half (47 per cent) of those considered for IP appeared in the Crown Court. Thirteen per cent had no previous convictions and 29 per cent had more than five (Table 6.2).

Table 6.2
Number of previous convictions

Number	n	%
None	23	(13)
1 to 5	107	(58)
6 to 10	42	(23)
Over 11	12	(6)
Total[1]	184	(100)

1 Information was unavailable for 3 referrals

Information on the most serious previous disposal (Table 6.3) shows that although referrals were young, two-fifths of them had served a custodial sentence in the past.

Table 6.3
Most serious previous disposal

Disposal	n	%
No Previous Disposal	23	(12)
YOI	76	(41)
Probation+4A/4B	4	(2)
Community Service	31	(17)
Probation	20	(11)
Attendance Centre	8	(4)
Fine/Compensation	19	(10)
Discharge	5	(3)
Total[1]	186	(100)

[1] Information was unavailable for 1 referral.

Half the referrals (51 per cent) had previously been convicted of a serious offence, the most serious previous offences including violence (16 per cent), a sex offence (one per cent), robbery (seven per cent) or a burglary in a dwelling (27 per cent).

Over a third (40 per cent) had been remanded in custody at some point prior to their court appearance, 27 per cent for the whole period and 13 per cent with a period of bail.

Table 6.4 shows the main offence for which offenders were referred for IP. Half (51 per cent) had been charged with a serious offence as defined above. These were evenly divided between violent offences (25 per cent) and burglary in a dwelling (26 per cent).

Table 6.4
Main offence at the time of referral

Offence	n	%
Violence	33	(18)
Sex Offence	2	(1)
Robbery	12	(6)
Burglary-Dwelling	48	(26)
Burglary-Other	22	(12)
Theft/Handling	21	(11)
TWOC/TADA	15	(8)
Fraud/Forgery	1	(1)
Drugs	3	(2)
Criminal Damage	3	(2)
Public Order	2	(1)
Indictable Motoring	20	(11)
Breach/Non-Payment	3	(2)
Other	2	(1)
Total	187	(100)

Half (51 per cent) had been charged with other offences in addition to the main offence and 12 per cent had more than five such offences.

As noted above, most referrals had previous convictions. Including those for whom the present offence was the first, the average age at first conviction was 16 years old.

From referral to sentence

In court, practically all defendants (98 per cent) pleaded guilty to the main offence. Most had been recommended for IP in their SIR, either on its own or with another recommendation (see Table 6.5).

Table 6.5
SIR recommendations

Recommended sentence	n	%
IP	134	(72)
CSO	16	(9)
IP+Others	19	(10)
Probation	7	(4)
Fine	2	(1)
Discharge	3	(2)
Other	1	(1)
No Recommendation	3	(2)
No SIR	2	(1)
Total	187	(100)

Most of those referred for IP were deemed acceptable (81 per cent). In total, 86 people (46 per cent) were sentenced to IP. This was in the form of probation plus a 4A or 4B requirement, probation plus a hostel requirement or straight probation. Table 6.6 shows the distribution of court disposals for all referrals. Nearly a third (31 per cent) received a custodial sentence for an average duration of 14 months.

Table 6.6
Court disposal

Disposal	n	%
YOI	58	(31)
Probation+4A/4B	56	(30)
Probation+Hostel Requirement	4	(2)
Community Service	19	(10)
Probation	40	(21)
Fine/Compensation	3	(2)
Discharge	5	(3)
Other	2	(1)
Total	187	(100)

So far, information following up offenders sentenced to IP has only been returned for eight people. Of these, three have completed successfully and five have had their order terminated due to reoffending.

Views of IP in the West Midlands

This section reports the views of magistrates, maingrade officers, senior managers and offenders who had been on intensive probation.

The views of magistrates

The West Midlands IP scheme was the largest in size and 771 questionnaires were sent to local magistrates; only 248 were returned, a response rate of 32 per cent. Of these responses, 136 (55 per cent) stated that they had heard of the IP scheme, although 11 said 'vaguely' and did not answer any further questions. Table 6.7 shows what the West Midlands magistrates thought the aims of the IP scheme were.

Table 6.7
Aims of the West Midlands IP project

Aim	Number of mentions
Alternative to/Reduce the use of custody	87
Treatment geared to the needs of the individual	22
Rehabilitation of offenders	15
Toughen up probation	14
Reduce offending	12
Tackle offending behaviour	12
Help with problems/needs of offenders	11
Increase options for the court	6
Other (inc. offer an intensive contract of work, more relevant for Crown Court)	4

By far the most common perceived aim of IP was to reduce the use of custody, but the next two most popular responses saw IP very much in social work terms and almost like the traditional probation order.

Magistrates' expectations about what offenders would do during their attendance at an IP scheme are set out in Table 6.8, and again social work activities seem to be seen as comprising the focus of intensive probation.

Table 6.8
What offenders might do on an IP scheme

Activity	Number of mentions
Examine offending behaviour	51
Group work	33
Community work	30
Comply with requirements/Co-operate	25
Tackle individual problems	25
Intensive supervision/monitoring	15
Learn acceptable behaviour	14
Learn to take responsibility	8
Receive help with employment	8
Use their time constructively	7
Other (inc. keep hands and minds occupied, help with substance abuse, raise self-esteem)	11

Tables 6.9 and 6.10 show the kind of offences for which magistrates thought they would use IP and the kind of offenders whom they might place on such a scheme.

Table 6.9
Offences for which IP might be used

Offence	Number of mentions
Drug/Alcohol related	62
Theft	32
Alternative to custody	31
Violence	28
Motoring	22
Sexual offences	21
Car theft	16
Burglary	15
Serious offences	11
Public order	10
Criminal damage	10
Deception	7
Other (inc. persistent non-violent offences, judged on merits of case, petty offences)	24

Table 6.10
Offenders who might be placed on IP

Offender	Number of mentions
17-20 year olds	38
Those at risk of custody	36
Those who are willing to change	34
Persistent offenders	24
Those who have failed on probation/CSO	10
17-25 year olds	7
Minor offenders	7
Those who need discipline	5
First time offenders	5
Those with behavioural problems (drink, drugs, anger)	5
Other (inc. those needing punishment and help, those from a deprived background, those who need help)	17

Unlike Leeds and Durham, drug and alcohol-related offences were overwhelmingly seen as the most appropriate for an IP programme. The kind of offenders who might be placed on IP were similar to those suggested by magistrates from the other two areas.

The West Midlands IP scheme had only been running for a few months when the questionnaires were sent to magistrates, and the form of the scheme was such that a specific place and programme were not easily identifiable; despite this, 16 per cent of those who had heard of the IP scheme claimed to have visited it.

Table 6.11 sets out magistrates' views about how IP might fit into the range of sentencing options. Once again, various views are evident about where IP fits into the sentencing structure; views which, if translated into practice, would lead to IP being used for offenders at different stages of their criminal careers.

Table 6.11
"How do you see IP fitting into the range of sentencing options available?"

Position	Number of mentions
Alternative to custody	35
Another option	31
"Very well"	11
Alternative to a community service order	6
Between probation and community service	6
More intensive than probation	5
For those with specific problems	4
Before community service	3
Between community service and custody	3
Other (inc. too early to say, between probation and detention centre, each case dealt with individually)	11

The possible advantages and disadvantages of IP are listed in Tables 6.12 and 6.13.

Table 6.12
Advantages of IP

Advantages	Number of mentions
Diversion from/Reduce the use of custody	31
Could reform/rehabilitate	23
Reduce offending	21
Focus on the individual	21
Tackles offending behaviour	14
Offers help/support for offenders	10
Another option	8
More demanding of the offender	7
Cost effective	6
Short but intensive	5
More control of offenders	4
Other (inc. reparation to the community, one-to-one relationship, better monitoring of progress)	13

Table 6.13
Disadvantages of IP

Disadvantages	Number of mentions
Offenders may see it as a soft option	34
Lack of trained probation officers	23
Must be run to the strictest standards	21
Public may see it as a soft option	15
Under-resourced	11
None	11
Offenders may not respond	9
Expensive	6
Risk of further offending as community-based	4
Very careful assessments needed	4
Other (inc. post-IP adjustment, too soon to say, no punishment involved, contamination)	17

The advantages are not seen to be in terms of improved control of offenders, but rather in better help being offered, and in general 'system' improvements (reducing use of prison and offending). Again, the main worry about IP is that offenders may see it as an easy option.

Other comments emphasised the need for sufficient resources to enable the project to be run properly; that monitoring and evaluation were vital; and that the programme had to be run strictly. That IP was a good thing and should be encouraged was mentioned often, although one magistrate did enquire "Weren't they supposed to be doing this already?"

The views of probation officers

Interviews were carried out with most of the field teams in the four divisions. There was considerable dissatisfaction expressed about the implementation and operation of IP in most of these teams. Problems with acceptance of the new initiative seemed to lead from two factors: first there was resistance to the whole notion of IP in some quarters – one officer referred to "fighting IP all the way". IP was seen as restricting probation officer autonomy, through introducing practice guidelines and Risk of Custody scales. It was also repeatedly described as "setting up offenders to fail": by imposing multiple requirements on young, chaotic offenders, it was felt that the inevitable outcome would be breach and custody. The other factor affecting the acceptance of the IP initiative has already been discussed in some detail: there was a very high degree of confusion surrounding the targeting, recommending and supervision of IP. The practice guidelines issued by senior management had not got through to field teams – or rather bits and pieces had got through, but other aspects of practice were completely misunderstood. A number of officers also complained that advice from senior management had changed during the course of the IP initiative – and this "changing of the goal posts" had contributed to the confusion. An example given here was the introduction and later withdrawal of the SIR paperwork.

Turning to individual interviews, in one team the SPO who had been largely responsible for its implementation in one field team left the office before the monitoring period was over. Although her replacement admitted he did not yet know what IP was, he knew that most probation officers did not like it and suspected that this was due to general resistance to high tariff disposals. However, only a handful of probation officers actually felt strongly against the introduction of such an order; most objected to the way in which it had been defined and implemented in the area, and to its lack of clarity. Probation officers in different teams, towards the end of the monitoring period, even believed it to be different things: some thought it was a replacement for 4A and/or 4B orders and others thought it was a replacement for all orders for people at risk of custody who were under 21. The lack of consistency in the field teams' understanding of the order meant that many different objections were voiced, depending on what form they thought the order took.

One of the officers' main objections was that they no longer had the option of recommending a straightforward conditional probation order since they had been instructed to recommend IP for anyone who would normally fall into this category. The main difference between IP and a conditional order as they saw it was that the former required weekly contact with a probation officer over a period of 6 months. As a result, offenders who needed to attend a group were automatically expected to report more frequently than they might otherwise have been. Several officers felt that, in this way, IP was being used as a replacement to 4A/4B orders rather than as an alternative to custody.

Along with the fear that they were targeting a low tariff group, many officers were reluctant to recommend an order which required such frequent contact as they did not believe the offenders would necessarily be able to maintain it. The inflexibility of the IP order also meant that breach proceedings were no longer at the discretion of the probation officer. As a result, officers would sometimes recommend a straight probation order with no conditions even if they thought the individual needed to do some sort of groupwork, rather than recommend an order which they considered would inevitably end in failure. An unintended effect of IP therefore was that the groupwork needs of offenders were not always being met. Some also thought that the high frequency of reporting was merely punitive rather than helpful.

As mentioned above, one factor which was resented by all probation officers across the field teams was the amount of extra paperwork they had to fill in when making a recommendation for IP. This consisted of three sections: the first specified the programme content, i.e. what the offender was going to do, and the frequency of contact, and stated that the individual understood the enforcement procedures. The second section consisted of an Action Plan which was essentially a summary of the first section, specifying what the offender would need to address and how he/she would do it. The third section was a contract which was signed by the probationer.

This paperwork was very much resented by probation officers who felt they were wasting a lot of time in order to achieve a probation order which was almost identical to what they could have achieved previously, but without the paperwork. One probation officer suggested that the extra paperwork also made the SIR less persuasive in court. This was due to the fact that the SIR conclusion would frequently refer the reader to the appendix which the court staff would not always have time to read.

Senior management's decision to abandon the paperwork, made towards the end of the monitoring period, was therefore met with a sigh of relief from maingrade officers and this change heralded the eventual demise of IP in the West Midlands. At this point, IP was being interpreted differently in each field team and by each probation officer. Some had reverted to making recommendations for conditional and straight probation orders without calling them "IP" whereas others were still calling all orders "IP" where they were for people under 21 who were at risk of custody. The 'death' of IP in the West Midlands was eagerly awaited by maingrade staff who generally felt that it had been a waste of time. A few argued that it had also been a waste of resources and that the money should have been used in the design of an additional high tariff order, such as STOP in Mid-Glamorgan. This, they felt, would have provided a genuine alternative to custody rather than dressing up existing orders with words such as "rigorous" and "intensive" just to sell them to the courts. One or two officers also suggested that IP would have been more successful had there been provision for out-reach work. This would have given the initiative an identity and might have had more impact on the target group.

A worrying criticism of IP that came up in interviews was the opinion that the service's credibility with the courts had suffered as a result of the confusion that surrounded its introduction. There were reports of sentencers being unsure how IP orders differed from probation orders with conditions. A magistrate had appeared at one probation office to ask about the progress of an offender who he thought was on IP, and it turned out that he was actually on a regular probation order. One confused magistrate had asked at a probation liaison committee meeting what the difference between an IP and a 4A/4B order was. The answer given was that there was no difference. When IP orders ceased to be available to the courts, many magistrates apparently were not informed and continued to request IP orders. These frequent misunderstandings and the general confusion surrounding IP cannot have helped the standing of the local service with the courts.

On the positive side, while the large majority of probation officers interviewed were critical of IP, some pointed to important lessons that had been learnt. A number of officers said that the IP initiative had successfully focused attention on the 17 to 20 year age group. This age group was very difficult to deal with, tending to live very chaotic life styles, having a lot of social and financial problems and a high rate of offending. As a result they tended to be a rather unpopular group with probation officers and IP had forced officers to give them special consideration. Another positive comment made was that IP had helped to increase standardisation across the four divisions and across individual teams: to quote an SPO, IP had "polished up practice a bit". While there had been much confusion over the CROC score ranges, the universal application of CROC scores had been a step in the right direction. While the paperwork was unpopular, it had led to more consistency of practice, and could have had a considerable effect on more wayward officers and teams. Lastly, it was stated that IP had led the service to be more aware of what the voluntary sector had to offer – and had moved probation officers another step towards becoming "managers of resources".

In summary, maingrade officers had generally felt confused about the precise aims of IP and about its structure which appeared to vary both between and within teams and which was redefined over time. As a result, there was much resentment towards senior managers who, it was argued, had mis-managed the situation and had caused them to waste considerable time and energy in an initiative which would eventually be abandoned. What positive remarks there were related to the issues of standardisation, working with the voluntary sector and targeting the needs of the 17 to 20 year age group.

The views of managers

To find out how senior management assessed the outcome of IP, semi-structured interviews were carried out with the DCPO and the ACPO who had been responsible for its management. In general, they too believed that IP had not been as successful as they had hoped; however, they attempted to draw some positive conclusions from it in the light of their objectives.

IP had been designed to fit in with an existing strategy to reduce custodial disposals in the West Midlands. Between 1989 and 1991, management had defined the three main objectives of this general strategy as follows: 1) to increase the proportion of community sentences, 2) to reduce the number of custodial sentences, and 3) to increase the tariff rating of people on community sentences, specifically 4A/4B orders.

While the existing strategy was implemented across the whole of the West Midlands, IP was only introduced to probation teams in the West of the county with the intention that it should complement the work already being done, rather than being a new disposal. Senior managers thought that the use of IP would make SIRs more consistent and make high tariff community disposals more attractive to the courts by way of the following factors: 1) the provision of offence focused SIRs with explicit and detailed recommendations; 2) the provision of explicit standards of contact and enforcement, which were shared with the court; 3) the use of voluntary organisations; 4) the use of probation resources across divisional boundaries; and 5) the offer of regular progress reports to the Courts. By implementing it in one half of the county only, they would be able to compare statistics from the two halves in order to see if it had enhanced their strategy.

The service published statistics on 17-20 year olds between 1989 and 1991. These showed that there was no difference between the two areas in terms of the first two objectives: both witnessed a substantial reduction in the absolute number of custodial disposals and a slight increase in the proportion of community disposals. Whereas the tariff scores of those who received 4A and 4B orders increased as hoped for in the non-IP areas, they were found to have actually decreased in the IP areas. Senior managers were disappointed in this latter outcome, but maintained that the decrease of the use of custody in the IP divisions could have been due to the introduction of the new order.

In discussing the confusion that surrounded the introduction of IP, the DCPO responsible thought that senior management may have underestimated the difficulty of ensuring consistency across the four divisions, and had also underestimated the difficulty of carrying the local union along with the IP initiative. Two weaknesses in the chain of communication had been the ACPO-SPO link and the SPO-field probation officer link. While the ACPO responsible for IP had done his best in informing his own SPOs about IP, the other ACPOs may not have done so well. Even where SPOs had received a clear picture of IP practice, many seemed unable to turn this into clear guidance which could be carried out by the probation officers in their teams.

The IP initiative was not helped by the fact that it appeared during a climate of professional resistance to Home Office led agendas, so that whatever management decided to do, they were bound to be seen as agents of the Home Office. IP was consequently regarded as being a more punitive form of probation and a way of imposing standards on discretionary professional practice. Another, albeit lesser, problem was that IP had been introduced at the same time as the Home Office funded two voluntary organisations in the area but maingrade staff were not consulted about working with them; as a result, many were concerned about the idea of voluntary bodies carrying out what they saw as being probation work. From a management point of view, working with voluntary bodies caused considerable problems due to the fact that they only had short-term funding, so it was impossible to plan ahead with much certainty.

On the brighter side, senior managers felt that there were some positive results. As a result of IP, there had been more consistent use of CROC scores and it was thought that fears of working with the voluntary sector had largely been abated. The demands of IP had also helped to set up day centres in Wolverhampton and Walsall and facilitate cross divisional use of resources.

IP also proved useful in paving the way for the new Criminal Justice Act 1991 in several ways. Firstly, there had been considerable professional debate about the meaning of "intensity" and this was expected to continue on the subject of "restriction of liberty". Secondly, the format of an IP referral in the SIR was similar to the format of pre-sentence reports required by the Act: both emphasised the current crime and called for a detailed description of the proposed community order. Thirdly, the setting of standards for probation programmes to some extent pre-empted the National Standards for the Supervision of Offenders in the Community (Home Office, 1992), particularly with respect to the enforcement of the order. Fourthly, both IP and the Act called for consistency in service provision, requiring the service to review its range of probation intervention and equality of opportunity and to engage with sentencers about the nature and detail of community orders. Finally, the Act specifies the importance of partnership and managers feel they have learnt a lot about working with the voluntary sector from their experience with IP.

In summary, senior management felt they had learnt a number of lessons from the exercise even though it had only been partially successful. They did regret the amount of anxiety and apprehension it had caused among maingrade staff, and better communication might have prevented some of this suffering.

The views of offenders

Only four offenders were available to be interviewed. This small number was due in part to problems arranging interviews: although the probation officers made an appointment for an interview to take place on the same day as a supervision session, the offender in question would often not turn up. Also, at this point, few offenders were actually on IP and most of those who had been on it had also finished their probation and could not be contacted.

Semi-structured interviews were ultimately carried out with two offenders who had finished their IP and were now on probation and two who were half-way through their IP. Three of them had been convicted of burglary offences and one of motoring offences. At the time of referral, none of them had heard of IP. One had been told by his probation officer that it was like probation but there was a group involved so it was a bit like doing a course. They had all been glad to get it rather than the custodial sentence they were expecting.

Two had been to an alcohol education group which they claimed had helped cut down their drinking. One had attended the motoring offenders group, and found it useful although he thought it should have been longer. Being unemployed, once it had finished he found he had too much time on his hands. Contact with the Rainer Foundation appeared to have been fruitful: two of them had found a job and a third had a job interview coming up.

All had enjoyed some element of IP, whether it was finding out that they were being helped with their problems or because the groupwork was enjoyable. IP was also valued as an alternative to custody due to the fact that they retained their freedom; one even preferred IP to probation because of the help he was given.

Summary

Intensive probation in the West Midlands proved to be rather different to the projects in Durham and Leeds. One cause of this divergence lay in the purpose behind the WMPS initiative, the chief aims of which were to increase standardisation and ensure uniform availability of high-tariff provision in four rather autonomous divisions. Perhaps unfortunately, these aims were largely unstated in the staff manual and the introductory letter sent to sentencers. Another important factor that differentiated IP in WMPS from IP elsewhere was that there was no physical centre for IP: no office and few specifically dedicated staff. The result of these factors was that IP took on a nebulous, insubstantial character, which was never dispelled. IP had a name, some headed paper (for a while) but little else to distinguish it from the high tariff orders that went before. While senior management could argue that this was their aim all along – IP was meant to be just an extension of good practice – for the officers who had to recommend this new order and for the magistrates that had to make this new order, the situation was thoroughly confused. This confusion may have been to some extent avoidable: as senior management pointed out, the chain of communication could have been better and used more often. Nevertheless, it would seem likely that, given its aims and the lack of a recognisable centre, the WMPS IP was always going to be somewhat ill-defined.

This is not to say that the initiative did not have its successes. In particular, some very important and unavoidable issues were addressed in the course of the implementation of IP. While many were not completely resolved over the course of the experiment with IP, the groundwork was laid for future developments. For instance, field teams began to recognise the potential for working with the voluntary sector. While resistance to this idea was not completely overcome, many officers were forced to re-evaluate what other agencies had to offer. The targeting of IP orders, however misconstrued, did lead to a reluctant acceptance of the use of CROC scores. While this may appear a little ill-timed, given that the Criminal Justice Act renders such scales obsolete, other targeting tools will be used and familiarity with using any such scale will prove helpful in the future. However, there are two important factors that must be weighed against the positive aspects of WMPS's experience of IP. First, the confusion and lack of direction experienced by field team probation officers must have led to some loss of faith in senior management. Second, there is the suggestion that sentencers may also have been confused by the introduction of a rather ill-defined new order and then its rapid disappearance. The image of the WMPS with sentencers may therefore have been affected as a result.

7 Conclusions

A considerable amount of data - both qualitative and quantitative - about intensive probation has been set out and discussed in the preceding chapters. This concluding chapter pulls together the main findings of the study and considers their significance. Given the wide-ranging nature of the evaluation this will not be an easy task. The approach adopted will involve splitting IP into four parts - the results of IP, issues relating to central policy development, local implementation issues, and the evaluation methodology. It should be emphasised that these are very much artificial distinctions - in practice the parts overlap and interact with each other.

The results of intensive probation

Viewed simply in terms of the number of offenders referred for intensive probation - 1,677 during the monitoring period - IP can be seen as successful. However, there are a few further points which may be worth considering in connection with this. First, these numbers may simply reflect a successful marketing strategy whereby local probation services successfully 'sold' the concept of IP to their staff. Second, many of these referrals are to IP programmes which represent only marginal changes to previously used day centres or 4A programmes. Third, there were wide variations amongst areas in the numbers referred; ranging from 17 in Greater Manchester (which only ran for 12 months) to 532 in West Yorkshire. And, of course, referrals are not always translated into sentences; of the 1,677 referrals to IP fewer than half (45 per cent) were sentenced to IP.

One of the objectives of the IP initiative was to try to ensure that both ethnic minority and female offenders were catered for. In the event, only five per cent (85) of referrals were for female offenders and almost half of these (40) came from the Newcastle IP scheme. The data on ethnic origin were not as reliable as they might have been due to some areas' refusal to use the OPCS categories on the monitoring form; in addition, there were 215 unspecified 'Other' cases, most of which seemed to have been completed instead of 'Don't Know'; and 39 missing cases. Of the 1,423 cases where a clear classification was made, 94 per cent were white, five per cent black and one per cent Asian. This represents a minimal figure for ethnic minority involvement in IP, but does suggest that in general IP schemes were dealing with ethnic minority offenders (in the absence of comprehensive local information it is difficult to be more precise, although it should be noted that at least one area had no ethnic minority referrals to IP).

In terms of the targeting of high-risk offenders for IP, schemes seemed to be successful: overall, only six per cent of referrals were for first offenders and 51 per cent had more than five previous convictions; 54 per cent of referrals had previous experience of custody; and 64 per cent were sentenced in the Crown Court. Risk assessment scores also suggested that referrals were, on the whole, at risk of a custodial sentence. The overall figures, however, mask some interesting variations. At one end of the spectrum, for the Gwent IP scheme 68 per cent of referrals had six or more previous convictions and the same proportion had served a custodial sentence; conversely, only 29 per cent of West Midlands referrals had six or more previous convictions, and 41 per cent had served a previous custodial sentence. Similarly, there were differences in the extent to which referrals were sentenced in the Crown Court, ranging from 35 per cent in Manchester (based on very few cases) and 39 per cent in Northumbria to 85 per cent in Hampshire.

Those who were sentenced to intensive probation were similar to those referred who were sentenced to other disposals in terms of their previous criminal history; but they did tend to be younger (56 per cent were under 21 compared to 44 per cent who did not get IP), to be less likely to be convicted of a violent offence (11 per cent compared to 17 per cent), they were more likely to be recommended for IP in a social inquiry report (84 per cent compared to 64 per cent) and were more likely to be sentenced in the magistrates' court (41 per cent compared to 32 per cent). The significance of a social inquiry report is, therefore, underlined but there is also a suggestion that it is more difficult to achieve an IP order at the Crown Court; 48 per cent of those dealt with at the Crown Court received custodial sentences compared to only 17 per cent of those dealt with at the magistrates' court. And it is instructive to compare the Crown Court and the magistrates' courts in terms of the sentencing of those who were referred for IP but did not get it; in the Crown Court 80 per cent received custodial sentences and eight per cent probation, whereas the magistrates' courts 34 per cent got custody and 34 per cent probation.

Sentencer satisfaction with IP seemed to be high (although it should be emphasised that was possible to interview very few judges). However, widely varying views about were propounded, which could not always be easily reconciled: IP was seen as an alternative to custody and at the same time expected to lead to a reduction in re-offending; there was little agreement about the position of IP amongst the sentencing options available to the courts; and relatively minor offences were mentioned as being suitable for IP. In general, the advantages of IP were seen as either system-oriented (reduce custody) or welfare-oriented (rehabilitation); any mention of the more punitive aspects of IP was rare. By far the major potential drawback of IP was identified as the possibility that offenders - or the public - might see it as a soft option.

Probation officers who worked on IP schemes were enthusiastic about them (with the exception of the West Midlands), and generally considered that they were doing positive work with high-risk offenders. Non-IP staff were not quite so enthusiastic, although this was dependent upon the length of time schemes had been running and the degree of consultation which had taken place. More negative comments centred upon the elitist nature of IP, the fact that more resources had been made available to IP when the same ends could be carried out by ordinary probation officers, and the use of voluntary organisations where staff were seen as unqualified and questions about breach were raised. It is notable that there were few criticisms of IP as overly controlling. The views of field staff could have an impact upon their referral rate to IP schemes and should not be ignored.

The views of offenders who participated in IP were very positive. There had been a feeling amongst probation staff opposed to IP that offenders would rebel against the rigorous requirements expected of them but, if anything, offenders appeared to enjoy and appreciate the attention which was given to them by their project workers. For the first time they felt that someone took a real interest in them and what they did. This was reflected in the remarkably positive comments made about their project workers (who were, for the most part, not professionally qualified probation officers). Unfortunately, due to the dominance of the project workers in their lives it seemed that the role of the probation officer was seen as less helpful; probation officers suffered by comparison with IP project workers. It is possible that this may have an effect upon the post-IP supervision.

Voluntary organisations were used in all IP schemes to a greater or lesser extent, but there was unease amongst probation officers about utilising such groups - an unease which could lead to anxieties amongst the voluntary organisations about their role in IP. Such unease was partly related to the history of working with other organisations. If this had been done for some time then there was less unhappiness amongst probation officers, but if it was a relatively new development it tended to be seen with suspicion. Such suspicions were fuelled by the publication in April 1990 of the discussion paper *Partnership in dealing with offenders in the Community* (Home Office 1990b) which was widely seen as a move by government to take away certain tasks from the probation service and move them to voluntary organisations. While there can be little doubt that tensions and resentments will continue about the respective roles of the probation service and the voluntary organisations, the IP initiative has shown that partnership schemes can work.

Contrary to the immediate perceptions of those opposed to IP, intensive probation was not only - indeed was rarely - about controlling offenders purely and simply. A great deal of social work was carried on under the aegis of IP schemes, and even where control could be seen as a dominant feature offenders were not at all unhappy about the demands made of them. IP schemes were not rigid and unchanging; they were flexible and could be adapted to changing circumstances. One possible problem was that of disengagement from IP; offenders might become so dependent upon frequent contact during IP that problems arise when they move on to the normal supervision part of their order. While IP staff were aware of this issue and efforts were made to combat its negative effects, there were few signs that successful strategies had been put into practice. Full involvement of field staff was essential for IP schemes, but all too often there remained a serious gap between IP and maingrade officers.

Finally, with respect to the results of IP, there is the question of IP's symbolic function. In these terms IP would seem to have been a success. It encouraged probation areas to think more carefully about demanding programmes for high-risk offenders, to be more responsive to the courts. Even in those areas where IP in practice was not particularly successful, it did begin to change attitudes or to uncover the kinds of problems which had to be tackled in order to provide more intensive forms of probation. Although hard data are not available, IP's contribution to culture change in probation should not be under-estimated.

Central policy development

It is regrettable that over the years so little attention has been paid by criminology to the development of policy and the impact that this has on criminal justice practice (but see Bottoms 1974, Downes 1988, Mair 1991, Rock 1990). All too often it seems to be assumed that policy initiatives are carefully and rationally prepared on the basis of in-depth knowledge about practice, and that these are unproblematically communicated to practitioners who then simply put them into practice. For a variety of reasons, this simple, rational model is rarely achieved in the real world. Policy is often developed reactively in response to a crisis; it may be formulated in a hurry without adequate knowledge or awareness of what is happening on the ground; policy has to be transmitted to various levels from the central policy-making body and at each one of these there is the possibility that the 'pure' policy may be diluted or changed to accord with local policy or practice (the greater the distance and the number of levels initiatives have to travel, the greater the chance that they can be subverted). Such issues can have a critical, though too often ignored, impact upon the success or failure of a policy and it is useful to address them in the context of intensive probation.

In the first place, IP was not best served by its initial incorporation into the 'Tackling Offending' initiative which immediately preceded it. There was some confusion amongst probation services about how IP was supposed to differ from the 'Tackling Offending' initiative - was it a separate development or a refinement of 'Tackling Offending'? Compounding the confusion was the timing of the IP initiative; if areas had been approached at the time of the 'Tackling Offending' initiative or a year or more later, rather than six months later, initial responses might have been more welcoming.

Certain assumptions seemed to be embedded in the IP policy initiative which were not borne out in practice and which may require reconsideration by those who formulate policy. A start date of 1 April 1990 for IP was only meaningful as a formal beginning of Home Office involvement; the areas which began IP on that date had been running a scheme for some time - and the length of time for which schemes had been running was an important factor in their success. Areas were not all at the same levels of development, either in terms of their own structures and organisations or in terms of their responses to government initiatives. Thus it took some areas a considerable time to get an IP scheme up and running - again with consequences for its success - and one area failed completely. Perhaps we assume too easily that probation areas are willing and able to develop and put into practice new programmes. Their willingness is affected by the desire to demonstrate that they are keen and ambitious (with a possible pay-off in terms of being viewed favourably when it comes to the allocation of resources). Nor will all areas have the will and the ability to develop new initiatives quickly and efficiently.

Home Office guidelines on the form of IP were vague, which had the advantage of allowing areas scope to develop their own ideas, but had the drawback of uncertainty about precisely what IP was all about. One example of this uncertainty can be seen in the way some IP schemes started life as responses to the 'Tackling Offending' initiative and were subsequently reinterpreted. Another interesting example of uncertainty at work is in the inclusion/exclusion/inclusion of South Yorkshire in the formal IP initiative. The confusion over the original plans to develop a further ten IP areas beginning in April 1991 also suggests a degree of uncertainty on behalf of the Home Office. In addition, there was no guidance for some considerable time on the status of IP once the combination order was introduced. Probation staff expressed unease at the time spent on developing IP when it might simply disappear on the arrival of the combination order.

Even where guidelines were reasonably clear - as in the requirement that IP should involve 4A or 4B conditions - these could be misunderstood or ignored by areas. The Newcastle IP scheme, ironically perhaps the most innovative, was a voluntary one but was not taken to task for this break from official guidelines. Similarly, the Greater Manchester IP scheme closed down 12 months early.

The issue of clarity versus ambiguity in policy has no easy answers; it is hard to strike the right balance between stating policy in general - and inevitably ambiguous - terms and in issuing clear, specific - but often inappropriate - instructions. But it is helpful to be clear about where ambiguity exists and why it is utilised. If one wishes to encourage experimental initiatives then ambiguity and vagueness are helpful, though again it should be noted that there is a price to pay in terms of trying to assess the worth of experimental social policy initiatives. In the first place, it is difficult and time-consuming to do properly; and secondly, it must be acknowledged that where experiments are concerned failure is as useful as success and expectations should not run ahead of reality.

One final point on the central policy aspect of IP. It should be noted that the IP initiative can be read as having an expressive or symbolic value which was, by its very nature, never clearly articulated. IP delivered a message to the probation service about the need to provide rigorous and demanding programmes which could successfully control high-risk offenders in the community. On this reading, IP is another push from central government to encourage the probation service to change direction and culture; and this is a move which has been going on since the early 1980s (the Statement of National Objectives and Priorities, the introduction of National Standards and of performance indicators can all be seen as examples of this trend).

Local implementation issues

Some of the issues falling under this heading have already been discussed in the previous section where relevant, but it is worth covering them again from a slightly different perspective.

If we take as the starting gate February 1989, when a Home Office letter went to the ten CPOs who were chosen as standard-bearers for IP, then some areas took up to 18 months to get their IP schemes underway. Those which met the start date were those which had been running IP under another name prior to the initiative. Even allowing for the fact that various groups would have to be consulted about proposals for IP (local NAPO branches seemed to be the most common) and that negotiations over detail might take some time, an 18 month time-lag between planning and practice seems to be rather lengthy. And, as has been pointed out previously, this meant that the IP programme would not have a full 24 months to run, which in turn had potential repercussions for the success of the programme.

It may be that probation areas need considerably more time or assistance to respond to requests from central government which involve what may be perceived as fairly radical shifts in practice. In retrospect, it is hard to underestimate the importance of having time to develop something like IP slowly and to learn from early mistakes. The West Yorkshire IP schemes provide a classic example of this; on the surface, they appeared not to have anything like the kind of problems found in the West Midlands, but it became clear that they too had had their problems - only they had faced these some years previously and managed to resolve most of the difficulties. It should be remembered that in studying initiatives such as IP, a good deal of what is found has to be interpreted in the context of a new programme - with the various advantages (such as staff enthusiasm for a new initiative) and disadvantages (such as unanticipated problems) which that may entail.

Another key factor in the local implementation process was the nature of the IP scheme itself; was it to be based in one location with a dedicated group of staff, or was it to be a general programme which could be applied by any maingrade officer? Other things being equal, setting up the former type of scheme would be a simpler matter than opting for the latter (although this is not to say that there are no problems associated with the former). Where the general option was followed, as in the West Midlands, the difficulties were exacerbated by the size of the area and the number of staff involved. Matters were further complicated by the fact that a local aim for IP was to encourage standardisation and consistency in the four divisions involved, which meant that it was unlikely that IP would be be practiced consistently for some time. Lack of effective communication between various levels of staff was another obstacle. Implementing IP in an area like the West Midlands (even allowing for the fact that only half of the area was included) was always going to pose problems, but by choosing the approach which was taken – which was, of course, dictated by local requirements – a rapid, effective implementation was always unlikely.

One advantage of a specific scheme with dedicated staff was that it tended to present messages about IP which were relatively clear and well-defined. Maingrade officers, whether they agreed with IP or not, at least knew where they stood with a specific scheme which had an office and staff. Again, one turns to the West Midlands experience to see how a more diffuse IP scheme could lead to considerable confusion and uncertainty amongst staff. Related to this point, is the need to differentiate IP from other probation programmes for high-risk offenders; something demonstrably new with a clearly defined target group was more likely to be successful in terms of attracting referrals from field staff and sentences from the courts. "Merely calling existing procedures by a new name is not enough to claim that implementation has occurred" (Palumbo et al. 1984), nor is it guaranteed to attract practitioners or sentencers.

Finally, in this section, it is worth commenting upon the lack of innovation in intensive probation programmes. This may have been due to a variety of factors, e.g. lack of ability to innovate, lack of time, confusion with other initiatives, lack of resources, reluctance to commit resources, fear of failure, the constraints of the then statutory framework, disagreement with the concept. Any or all of these might apply to individual areas but essentially they suggest that a conducive atmosphere or framework for innovation did not exist. And, of course, it has already been noted that the one innovatory scheme (Newcastle) chose to situate itself outside of the formal guidelines for IP.[1]

The evaluation methodology

On the whole the evaluation methodology used worked well. It involved much more work than the more traditional approach of describing the scheme/programme as it was planned and measuring recidivism. And it has provided a much more complex set of data by which to assess the outcome of intensive probation. It has also, however, addressed the point made by Harland and Harris (1984, 1987) about the lack of process studies in criminal justice research and how this cripples new developments. It has confirmed the findings of Musheno and his colleagues (1989) about the significance of organisational conditions for the implementation of policy. The IP evaluation has shown quite clearly that the process by which policy is developed, transmitted to probation chief officers and then translated into practice is of critical importance not only in its own right, but in terms of its impact upon the workings – and thus the outcomes – of IP. It has also demonstrated again that to look at a disposal globally may mask key differences amongst various forms of that disposal (cf. Mair and Nee 1992).

---

[1] It is interesting to note in the context of central policy development and local implementation the moves which are being encouraged by the National Institute of Corrections in the USA with the publication of reports on such subjects as *Marketing Community Corrections* (1988), *Managing the Development of Community Corrections* (1990) and *The Practical Planning Guide for Community Corrections Managers* (1991). It should also be noted that the development of National Standards for supervision in the community was very much a collaborative effort between policy makers and practitioners.

The study was not as successful as it might have been in collecting data on the costs of IP, and on the secondary outcome measures proposed. Few probation areas are yet in a position to assess the costs of specific parts of their work, although this may change as the Resource Management Information System begins to be implemented. Similarly, areas may have held information about the extent to which offender problems such as accommodation, employment, drug misuse and the like were successfully tackled, but they were not held in a form which was easily accessible to researchers.

This approach to evaluation does not provide simple answers, but it does reflect much more accurately the complex nature of the phenomenon being evaluated. It highlights the absurdity of asking a question such as 'What works ?' with its naive, simplistic assumptions. IP worked well in some areas and not so well in others; it worked well in some manifestations and not so well in others. Given the nature of the initiative, this is the kind of result which might have been expected but which a narrow approach to evaluation would have obscured.

*   *   *

To sum up briefly a study of this kind is not easy, but taking account of the various – and not always compatible – objectives of IP, the experimental nature of the IP initiative, and the fact that success (like implementation) is a matter of degree and not an all or nothing judgement (Palumbo et al. 1984), then IP must on the evidence presented in this report be judged to have been reasonably successful. A further publication will consider the two key areas of recidivism and sentencing trends in IP areas.

References

Audit Commission. (1989). *The Probation Service: promoting value for money.* London: HMSO

Bale, D. (1989). 'The Cambridgeshire Risk of Custody scale'. In: Mair, G. (Ed.), *Risk Prediction and Probation: papers from a Research and Planning Unit workshop.* RPU Paper 56. London: Home Office.

Bottomley, A.K., James, A., Bochel, C. and Robinson, D-M. (1992). *A Study of the probation service response to the 'Tackling Offending' initiative.* University of Hull: Centre for Criminology and Criminal Justice.

Bottoms, A.E. (1974). 'On the decriminalisation of English juvenile courts'. In: Hood R. (Ed), *Crime, Criminology and Public Policy: essays in honour of Sir Leon Radzliowicz.* London: Heinemann.

Brody, S.R. (1976). *The Effectiveness of Sentencing: a review of the literature.* Home Office Research Study No.35. London: HMSO

Brownlee, I.D. and Joanes, D. (1992). *Leeds Young Adult Offenders Project: a third evaluation report.* London: National Children's Home.

Byrne, J.M., Lurigio, A.J. and Petersilia, J. (Eds.) (1992). *Smart Sentencing: the emergence of intermediate sanctions.* Newbury Park, Ca: Sage.

Crime and Delinquency, (1990). 36: 3-191.

DHSS (1983). *Further developments in Intermediate Treatment.* Local Authority Circular No. 83-3.

Downes, D. (1988). *Constraints in Tolerance: post-war penal policy in the Netherlands and England and Wales.* Oxford: Clarendon Press.

Federal Probation, (1986). 50: 1-81.

Folkard, M.S. *et al.* (1974). *IMPACT Vol.I: the design of the probation experiment and an interim evaluation.* Home Office Research Study No.24. London: HMSO

Folkard, M.S., Smith, D.E. and Smith, D.D. (1976). *IMPACT Vol.II: the results of the experiment.* Home Office Research Study No.36. London: HMSO

Godson, D., Cureton, L. and Swyer, B. (1991). *Probation Centres Observed.* Hampshire Probation Service Information and Research Unit.

Haller, S. and Mullaney, F.G. (1988). *Marketing Community Corrections.* Washington, DC: US Department of Justice, National Institute of Corrections.

Harland, A.T. and Harris, P.W. (1984). 'Developing and implementing alternatives to incarceration: a problem of planned change in criminal justice'. *University of Illinois Law Review*, 319-364.

Harland, A.T. and Harris, P.W. (1987). 'Structuring the development of alternatives to incarceration'. In: Gottfedson, S.D. and McConville, S. (Eds.), *America's Correctional Crisis: prison populations and public policy.* New York: Greenwood Press.

Hedderman, C. (1991). 'Custody decisions for property offenders in the Crown Court'. *The Howard Journal of Criminal Justice*, 30: 207-217.

Home Office. (1988a). *Punishment, Custody and the Community.* Cm 424. London: HMSO

Home Office. (1988b). *Tackling Offending: an action plan.* London: Home Office.

Home Office. (1990a). *Crime, Justice abd Protecting the Public.* Cm 965. London: HMSO

Home Office. (1990b). *Partnership in dealing with offenders in the community.* London: Home Office.

Home Office. (1991). *Report of the Work of the Prison Service, April 1990 – March 1991.* Cm 1724. London: HMSO

Home Office. (1992a). *Prison Statistics England and Wales 1990.* Cm 1800. London: HMSO

Home Office. (1992b). *Criminal Statistics England and Wales 1990.* Cm 1935. London: HMSO

Home Office. (1992c). *National Standards for the supervision of offenders in the community.* London: HMSO

Home Office. (1993). *Probation Statistics England and Wales 1991.* London: Home Office.

Larivee, J.J. and O'Leary, W.D. (1990). *Managing the Development of Community Corrections.* Washington, DC: US Department of Justice, National Institute of Corrections.

McCarthy, B.R. (Ed.) (1987). *Intermediate Punishments: intensive supervision, home confinement and electronic surveillance.* Monsey, NY: Criminal Justice Press.

Mair, G. (1991). *Part Time Punishment ? The origins and development of senior attendance centres.* London: HMSO

Mair, G. and Nee, C. (1992). 'Day centre reconviction rates'. *British Journal of Criminology*, 32: 329-339.

Musheno, M.C., Palumbo, D.J., Maynard-Moody, S. and Levine, J.P. (1989). 'Community corrections as an organizational innovation: what works and why'. *Journal of Research in Crime and Delinquency*, 26: 136-167.

Palumbo, D.J., Maynard-Moody, S. and Wright, P. (1984). 'Measuring degrees of successful implementation: achieving policy versus statutory goals'. *Evaluation Review*, 8: 45-74

Petersilia, J. (1987). *Expanding Options for Criminal Sentencing.* Santa Monica, Ca: RAND.

Petersilia, J. and Turner, S. (1991). 'An evaluation of intensive probation in California'. *The Journal of Criminal Law and Criminology*, 82: 610-658.

The Practical Planning Guide for Community Corrections Managers. (1991). Washington, DC: US Department of Justice, National Institute of Corrections.

Roberts, C. (1990). 'Nothing Works Re-Assessed: the effectiveness of forms of probation supervision on subsequent criminal careers'. Paper presented to the ACOP Finance and Resources Group Seminar.

Rock, P. (1990). *Helping Victims of Crime: The Home Office and the rise of victim support in England and Wales.* Oxford: Clarendon Press.

Publications

The Research and Planning Unit (previously the Research Unit) has been publishing its work since 1955, and a full list of Papers is provided below. These reports are available on request from the Home Office Research and Planning Unit, Information Section, Room 278, 50 Queen Anne's Gate, London SW1H 9AT. Telephone: 071-273 2084 (answerphone).

Reports published in the HORS series are available from HMSO, who will advise as to prices, at the following address: :

HMSO Publications Centre
PO Box 276
London SW8 5DT

Telephone orders: 071-873 9090

General enquiries: 071-873 0011

Titles already published for the Home Office

Studies in the Causes of Delinquency and the Treatment of Offenders (SCDTO)

1.   Prediction methods in relation to borstal training. Hermann Mannheim and Leslie T. Wilkins. 1955. viii + 276pp. (11 340051 9)

2.   Time spent awaiting trial. Evelyn Gibson. 1960. v + 45pp. (34-368-2).

3.   Delinquent generations. Leslie T. Wilkins. 1960. iv + 20pp. (11 340053 5).

4.   Murder. Evelyn Gibson and S. Klein. 1961. iv + 44pp. (11 340054 3).

5.   Persistent criminals. A study of all offenders liable to preventive detention in 1956. W.H. Hammond and Edna Chayen. 1963. ix + 237pp.(34-368-5).

6.   Some statistical and other numerical techniques for classifying individuals. P.McNaughton-Smith. 1965. v + 33pp (34-368-6).

7.   Probation research: a preliminary report. Part I. General outline of research. Part II. Study of Middlesex probation area (SOMPA) Steven Folkard, Kate Lyon, Margaret M. Carver and Erica O'Leary. 1966.vi + 58pp. (11 340374 7).

8.   Probation research: national study of probation. Trends and regional comparisons in probation (England and Wales). Hugh Barr and Erica O'Leary. 1966. vii + 51pp. (34-368-8).

9.   Probation research. A survey of group work in the probation service. Hugh Barr. 1966. vii + 94pp. (34-368-9).

10.   Types of delinquency and home background. A validation study of Hewitt and Jenkins' hypothesis. Elizabeth Field. 1967. vi + 21pp. (34-368-10).

11. Studies of female offenders. No. 1 - Girls of 16-20 years sentenced to borstal or detention centre training in 1963. No. 2 - Women offenders in the Metropolitan Police District in March and April 1957. No. 3 - A description of women in prison on January 1, 1965. Nancy Goodman and Jean Price. 1967. v + 78pp. (34-368-11).

12. The use of the Jesness Inventory on a sample of British probationers. Martin Davies. 1967. iv + 20pp. (34-368-12).

13. The Jesness Inventory: application to approved school boys. Joy Mott. 1969. iv + 27pp. (11 340063 2).

Home Office Research Studies (HORS)

(Nos 1–106 are out of print)

1. Workloads in children's departments. Eleanor Grey. 1969. vi + 75pp. (11 340101 9).

2. Probationers in their social environment. A study of male probationers aged 17-20, together with an analysis of those reconvicted within twelve months. Martin Davies. 1969. vii + 204pp. (11 340102 7).

3. Murder 1957 to 1968. A Home Office Statistical Division report on murder in England and Wales. Evelyn Gibson and S. Klein (with annex by the Scottish Home and Health Department on murder in Scotland). 1969. vi + 94pp. (11 340103 5).

4. Firearms in crime. A Home Office Statistical Division report on indictable offences involving firearms in England and Wales. A. D. Weatherhead and B. M. Robinson. 1970. viii + 39pp. (11 340104 3).

5. Financial penalties and probation. Martin Davies. 1970. vii + 39pp. (11 340105 1).

6. Hostels for probationers. A study of the aims, working and variations in effectiveness of male probation hostels with special reference to the influence of the environment on delinquency. Ian Sinclair. 1971.x + 200pp. (11 340106 X).

7. Prediction methods in criminology - including a prediction study of young men on probation. Frances H. Simon. 1971. xi + 234pp.(11 340107 8).

8. Study of the juvenile liaison scheme in West Ham 1961-65. Marilyn Taylor. 1971. vi + 46pp. (11 340108 6).

9. Explorations in after-care. I - After-care units in London, Liverpool and Manchester. Martin Silberman (Royal London Prisoners' Aid Society) and Brenda Chapman. II - After-care hostels receiving a Home Office grant. Ian Sinclair and David Snow (HORU). III - St. Martin of Tours House, Aryeh Leissner (National Bureau for Co-operation in Child Care). 1971. xi + 140pp. (11 340109 4).

10. A survey of adoption in Great Britain. Eleanor Grey in collaboration with Ronald M. Blunden. 1971. ix + 168pp. (11 340110 8).

11. Thirteen-year-old approved school boys in 1960s. Elizabeth Field, W H Hammond and J. Tizard. 1971.ix + 46pp. (11 340111 6).

12. Absconding from approved schools. R. V. G. Clarke and D. N. Martin. 1971. vi + 146pp.(11 340112 4).

13. An experiment in personality assessment of young men remanded in custody. H. Sylvia Anthony. 1972. viii + 79pp. (11 340113 2).

14. Girl offenders aged 17-20 years. I - Statistics relating to girl offenders aged 17-20 years from 1960 to 1970. II - Re-offending by girls released from borstal or detention centre training. III - The problems of girls released from borstal training during their period on after-care. Jean Davies and Nancy Goodman. 1972. v + 77pp. (11 340114 0).

15. The controlled trial in institutional research - paradigm or pitfall for penal evaluators? R. V. G. Clarke and D. B. Cornish. 1972. v + 33pp. (11 340115 9).

16. A survey of fine enforcement. Paul Softley. 1973. v + 65pp. (11 340116 7).

17. An index of social environment - designed for use in social work research. Martin Davies. 1973. vi + 63pp. (11 340117 5).

18. Social enquiry reports and the probation service. Martin Davies and Andrea Knopf. 1973. v + 49pp.(11 340118 3).

19. Depression, psychopathic personality and attempted suicide in a borstal sample. H. Sylvia Anthony.1973. viii + 44pp. (0 11 340119 1).

20. The use of bail and custody by London magistrates' courts before and after the Criminal Justice Act 1967. Frances Simon and Mollie Weatheritt. 1974. vi + 78pp. (0 11 340120 5).

21. Social work in the environment.A study of one aspect of probation practice. Martin Davies, with Margaret Rayfield, Alaster Calder and Tony Fowles. 1974. ix + 151pp. (0 11 340121 3).

22. Social work in prison. An experiment in the use of extended contact with offenders. Margaret Shaw.1974. viii + 154pp. (0 11 340122 1).

23. Delinquency amongst opiate users. Joy Mott and Marilyn Taylor. 1974.vi + 31pp. (0 11 340663 0).

24. IMPACT. Intensive matched probation and after-care treatment. Vol. I - The design of the probation experiment and an interim evaluation. M. S. Folkard, A. J. Fowles, B.C. McWilliams, W. McWilliams, D. D. Smith, D. E. Smith and G. R. Walmsley. 1974. v + 54pp. (0 11 340664 9).

25. The approved school experience. An account of boys' experiences of training under differing regimes of approved schools,with an attempt to evaluate the effectiveness of that training. Anne B. Dunlop. 1974. vii + 124pp. (0 11 340665 7).

26. Absconding from open prisons. Charlotte Banks, Patricia Mayhew and R. J. Sapsford. 1975. viii + 89pp. (0 11 340666 5).

27. Driving while disqualified. Sue Kriefman. 1975. vi + 136pp.(0 11 340667 3).

28. Some male offenders' problems. - Homeless offenders in Liverpool. W. McWilliams. II - Casework with short-term prisoners. Julie Holborn. 1975. x + 147pp. (0 11 340668 1).

29. Community service orders. K. Pease, P. Durkin, I. Earnshaw, D. Payne and J. Thorpe. 1975. viii + 80pp.(0 11 340669 X).

30. Field Wing Bail Hostel: the first nine months. Frances Simon and Sheena Wilson. 1975. viii + 55pp. (0 11 340670 3).

31. Homicide in England and Wales 1967-1971. Evelyn Gibson. 1975. iv + 59pp. (0 11 340753 X).

32. Residential treatment and its effects on delinquency. D. B. Cornish and R. V. G. Clarke. 1975. vi + 74pp. (0 11 340672 X).

33. Further studies of female offenders. Part A: Borstal girls eight years after release. Nancy Goodman, Elizabeth Maloney and Jean Davies. Part B: The sentencing of women at the London Higher Courts. Nancy Goodman, Paul Durkin and Janet Halton. Part C: Girls appearing before a juvenile court. Jean Davies. 1976. vi + 114pp. (0 11 340673 8).

34. Crime as opportunity. P. Mayhew, R. V. G. Clarke, A. Sturman and J. M. Hough. 1976. vii + 36pp.(0 11 340674 6).

35. The effectiveness of sentencing: a review of the literature. S. R. Brody. 1976. v + 89pp.(0 11 340675 4).

36. IMPACT. Intensive matched probation and after-care treatment. Vol. II - The results of the experiment. M. S. Folkard, D. E. Smith and D. D. 1976. xi + 40pp. (0 11 340676 2).

37. Police cautioning in England and Wales. J. A. Ditchfield. 1976. v + 31pp. (0 11 340677 0).

38. Parole in England and Wales. C. P. Nuttall, with E. E. Barnard, A. J. Fowles, A. Frost, W. H. Hammond, P. Mayhew, K. Pease, R. Tarling and M. J. Weatheritt. 1977. vi + 90pp. (0 11 340678 9).

39. Community service assessed in 1976. K. Pease, S. Billingham and I. Earnshaw. 1977. vi + 29pp.(0 11 340679 7).

40. Screen violence and film censorship: a review of research. Stephen Brody. 1977. vii + 179pp.(0 11 340680 0).

41. Absconding from borstals. Gloria K. Laycock. 1977. v + 82pp. (0 11 340681 9).

42. Gambling: a review of the literature and its implications for policy and research. D. B. Cornish. 1978.xii + 284pp. (0 11 340682 7).

43. Compensation orders in magistrates' courts. Paul Softley. 1978. v + 41pp. (0 11 340683 5).

44. Research in criminal justice. John Croft. 1978. iv + 16pp. (0 11 340684 3).

45. Prison welfare: an account of an experiment at Liverpool. A. J. Fowles. 1978. v + 34pp. (0 11 340685 1).

46. Fines in magistrates' courts. Paul Softley. 1978. v + 42pp. (0 11 340686 X).

47. Tackling vandalism. R. V. Clarke (editor), F. J. Gladstone, A. Sturman and Sheena Wilson 1978. vi + 91pp. (0 11 340687 8).

48. Social inquiry reports: a survey. Jennifer Thorpe. 1979. vi + 55pp. (0 11 340688 6).

49. Crime in public view. P. Mayhew, R. V. G. Clarke, J. N. Burrows, J. M. Hough and S. W. C. Winchester. 1979. v + 36pp. (0 11 340689 4).

50. Crime and the community. John Croft. 1979. v + 16pp. (0 11 340690 8).

51. Life-sentence prisoners. David Smith (editor), Christopher Brown, Joan Worth, Roger Sapsford and Charlotte Banks (contributors). 1979. iv + 51pp. (0 11 340691 6).

52. Hostels for offenders. Jane E. Andrews, with an appendix by Bill Sheppard. 1979. v + 30pp. (0 11 340692 4).

53. Previous convictions, sentence and reconviction: a statistical study of a sample of 5,000 offenders convicted in January 1971. G. J. O. Phillpotts and L. B. Lancucki. 1979. v + 55pp. (0 11 340693 2).

54. Sexual offences, consent and sentencing. Roy Walmsley and Karen White. 1979. vi + 77pp.(0 11 340694 0).

55. Crime prevention and the police. John Burrows, Paul Ekblom and Kevin Heal. 1979. v + 37pp. (0 11 340695 9).

56. Sentencing practice in magistrates' courts. Roger Tarling, with the assistance of Mollie Weatheritt. 1979. vii + 54pp. (0 11 340696 7).

57. Crime and comparative research. John Croft. 1979. iv + 16pp. (0 11 340697 5).

58. Race, crime and arrests. Philip Stevens and Carole F. Willis. 1979. v + 69pp. (0 11 340698 3).

59. Research and criminal policy. John Croft. 1980. iv + 14pp. (0 11 340699 1).

60. Junior attendance centres. Anne B. Dunlop. 1980. v + 47pp. (0 11 340700 9).

61. Police interrogation: an observational study in four police stations. Paul Softley, with the assistance of David Brown, Bob Forde, George Mair and David Moxon. 1980. vii + 67pp. (0 11 340701 7).

62. Co-ordinating crime prevention efforts. F. J. Gladstone. 1980. v + 74pp. (0 11 340702 5).

63. Crime prevention publicity: an assessment. D. Riley and P. Mayhew. 1980. v + 47pp.(0 11 340703 3).

64. Taking offenders out of circulation. Stephen Brody and Roger Tarling. 1980. v + 46pp.(0 11 340704 1).

65. Alcoholism and social policy: are we on the right lines? Mary Tuck. 1980. v + 30pp. (0 11 340705 X).

66. Persistent petty offenders. Suzan Fairhead. 1981. vi + 78pp. (0 11 340706 8).

67.   Crime control and the police. Pauline Morris and Kevin Heal. 1981. v + 71pp. (0 11 340707 6).

68.   Ethnic minorities in Britain: a study of trends in their position since 1961. Simon Field, George Mair, Tom Rees and Philip Stevens. 1981. v + 48pp. (0 11 340708 4).

69.   Managing criminological research. John Croft. 1981. iv + 17pp. (0 11 340709 2).

70.   Ethnic minorities, crime and policing: a survey of the experiences of West Indians and whites. Mary Tuck and Peter Southgate. 1981. iv + 54pp. (0 11 340765 3).

71.   Contested trials in magistrates' courts. Julie Vennard. 1982. v + 32pp. (0 11 340766 1).

72   Public disorder: a review of research and a study in one inner city area. Simon Field and Peter Southgate. 1982. v + 77pp. (0 11 340767 X).

73.   Clearing up crime. John Burrows and Roger Tarling. 1982. vii + 31pp. (0 11 340768 8).

74.   Residential burglary: the limits of prevention. Stuart Winchester and Hilary Jackson. 1982. v + 47pp. (0 11 340769 6).

75.   Concerning crime. John Croft. 1982. iv + 16pp. (0 11 340770 X).

76.   The British Crime Survey: first report. Mike Hough and Pat Mayhew. 1983. v + 62pp. (0 11 340786 6).

77.   Contacts between police and public: findings from the British Crime Survey. Peter Southgate and Paul Ekblom. 1984. v + 42pp. (0 11 340771 8).

78.   Fear of crime in England and Wales. Michael Maxfield. 1984. v + 57pp. (0 11 340772 6).

79.   Crime and police effectiveness. Ronald V Clarke and Mike Hough 1984. iv + 33pp. (0 11 340773 3).

80.   The attitudes of ethnic minorities. Simon Field. 1984. v + 49pp. (0 11 340774 2).

81.   Victims of crime: the dimensions of risk. Michael Gottfredson. 1984. v + 54pp. (0 11 340775 0).

82.   The tape recording of police interviews with suspects: an interim report. Carole Willis.1984.v + 45pp.(0 11 340776 9).

83.   Parental supervision and juvenile delinquency. David Riley and Margaret Shaw. 1985.v + 90pp.(0 11 340799 8).

84.   Adult prisons and prisoners in England and Wales 1970-1982: a review of the findings of social research. Joy Mott. 1985. vi + 73pp. (0 11 340801 3).

85.   Taking account of crime: key findings from the 1984 British Crime Survey. Mike Hough and Pat Mayhew. 1985. vi + 115pp. (0 11 341810 2).

86.   Implementing crime prevention measures. Tim Hope. 1985. vi + 82pp. (0 11 340812 9).

87. Resettling refugees: the lessons of research. Simon Field. 1985. vi + 66pp.
     (0 11 340815 3).

88. Investigating burglary: the measurement of police performance. John Burrows.
     1986. vi + 36pp.(0 11 340824 2)

89. Personal violence. Roy Walmsley. 1986. vi + 87pp. (0 11 340827 7).

90. Police-public encounters. Peter Southgate. 1986. vi + 150pp. (0 11 340834 X).

91. Grievance procedures in prisons. John Ditchfield and Claire Austin. 1986. vi + 87pp.
     (0 11 340839 0).

92. The effectiveness of the Forensic Science Service. Malcolm Ramsay. 1987.
     v + 100pp.(0 11 340842 0).

93. The police complaints procedure: a survey of complainant's views. David Brown.
     1987. v + 98pp. (0 11 340853 6).

94. The validity of the reconviction prediction score. Denis Ward. 1987. vi + 46.
     (0 11 340882 X).

95. Economic aspects of the illicit drug market enforcement policies in the United
     Kingdom. Adam Wagstaff and Alan Maynard. 1988. vii + 156pp. (0 11 340883 8)

96. Schools, disruptive behaviour and deliquency: a review of literature. John Graham.
     1988. v + 70pp. (0 11 340887 0).

97. The tape recording of police interviews with suspects: a second interim report.
     Carole Willis, John Macleod and Peter Naish. 1988. vii + 97pp. (011 340890 0).

98. Triable-either-way cases: Crown Court or magistrate's court. David Riley and Julie
     Vennard. 1988. v + 52pp. (0 11 340891 9).

99. Directing patrol work: a study of uniformed policing. John Burrows and Helen
     Lewis. 1988 v + 66pp. (0 11 340891 9)

100. Probation day centres. George Mair. 1988. v + 44pp. (0 11 340894 3).

101. Amusement machines: dependency and delinquency. John Graham. 1988. v + 48pp.
     (0 11 340895 1).

102. The use and enforcement of compensation orders in magistrates' courts. Tim
     Newburn. 1988. v + 49pp. (0 11 340 896 X)

103. Sentencing practice in the Crown Court. David Moxon. 1988. v + 90pp.
     (0 11 340902 8).

104. Detention at the police station under the Police and Criminal Evidence Act 1984.
     David Brown. 1988. v + 88pp. (0 11340908 7).

105. Changes in rape offences and sentencing. Charles Lloyd and Roy Walmsley. 1989.
     vi + 53pp.(0 11 340910 9).

106. Concerns about rape. Lorna Smith. 1989. v + 48pp. (0 11 340911 7).

107. Domestic violence. Lorna Smith. 1989. v + 132pp. (0 11 340925 7)

108. Drinking and disorder: a study of non-metropolitan violence. Mary Tuck. 1989. v + 111pp. (011 340926 5).

109. Special security units. Roy Walmsley. 1989. v + 114pp. (0 11 340961 3).

110. Pre-trial delay: the implications of time limits. Patricia Morgan and Julie Vennard. 1989. v + 66pp. (0 11 340964 8)

111. The 1988 British Crime Survey. Pat Mayhew, David Elliott and Lizanne Dowds. 1989. v + 133pp. (0 11 340965 6).

112. The settlement of claims at the Criminal Injuries Compensation Board. Tim Newburn. 1989. v + 40pp. (0 11 340967 2)

113. Race, community groups and service delivery. Hilary Jackson and Simon Field. 1989. v + 62pp.(0 11 340972 9)

114. Money payment supervision orders: probation policy and practice. George Mair and Charles Lloyd. 1989.v + 40pp. (0 11 340971 0).

115. Suicide and self-injury in prison: a literature review. Charles Lloyd. 1990. v + 69pp. (0 11 3409745 5).

116. Keeping in Touch: police-victim communication in two areas. Tim Newburn and Susan Merry. 1990. v + 52pp. (0 11 340974 5).

117. The police and public in England and Wales: a British Crime Survey report. Wesley G. Skogan. 1990. vi + 74pp. (0 11 340995 8).

118. Control in prisons: a review of the literature. John Ditchfield. 1990 (0 11 340996 6).

119. Trends in crime and their interpretation: a study of recorded crime in post-war England and Wales. Simon Field. 1990. (0 11 340994 X).

120. Electronic monitoring: the trials and their results. George Mair and Claire Nee. 1990. v + 79pp (0 11 340998 2).

121. Drink driving: the effects of enforcement. David Riley. 1991. viii + 78pp (0 11 340999 0).

122. Managing difficult prisoners: the Parkhurst Special Unit. Roy Walmsley (Ed.) 1991. x + 139pp (0 11 341008 5).

123. Investigating burglary: the effects of PACE. David Brown. 1991. xii + 106pp. (0 11 341011 5).

124. Traffic policing in changing times. Peter Southgate and Catriona Mirrlees-Black. 1991. viii + 139pp (0 11 341019 0)

125. Magistrates' court or Crown Court ? Mode of trial decisions and sentencing. Carol Hedderman and David Moxon. 1992. vii + 53pp. (0 11 341036 0).

126. Developments in the use of compensation orders in magistrates' courts since October 1988. David Moxon, John Martin Corkery and Carol Hedderman. 1992. x + 48pp. (0 11 341042 5).

127. A comparative study of firefighting arrangements in Britain, Denmark, the Netherlands and Sweden. John Graham, Simon Field, Roger Tarling and Heather Wilkinson. 1992. x + 57pp. (0 11 341043 3).

128. The National Prison Survey 1991: main findings. Roy Walmsley, Liz Howard and Sheila White. 1992. xiv + 82pp. (0 11 341051 4).

129. Changing the Code: police detention under the revised PACE Codes of Practice. David Brown, Tom Ellis and Karen Larcombe. 1992. viii + 122pp. (0 11 341052 2).

130. Car theft: the offender's perspective. Roy Light, Claire Nee and Helen Ingham. 1993. x + 89pp. (0 11 341069 7).

131. Housing, Community and Crime: The Impact of the Priority Estates Project. Janet Foster and Timothy Hope with assistance from Lizanne Dowds and Mike Sutton. 1993. xi + 118. (0 11 341078 6).

132. The 1992 British Crime Survey. Pat Mayhew, Natalie Aye Maung and Catriona Mirrlees-Black. 1993. xiii + 206. (0 11 341094 8).

Research and Planning Unit Papers (RPUP)

1. Uniformed police work and management technology. J. M. Hough. 1980.

2. Supplementary information on sexual offences and sentencing. Roy Walmsley and Karen White. 1980.

3. Board of visitor adjudications. David Smith, Claire Austin and John Ditchfield. 1981.

4. Day centres and probation. Suzan Fairhead, with the assistance of J.Wilkinson-Grey. 1981.

5. Ethnic minorities and complaints against the police. Philip Stevens and Carole Willis. 1982.

6. Crime and public housing. Mike Hough and Pat Mayhew (editors). 1982.

7. Abstracts of race relations research. George Mair and Philip Stevens (editors). 1982.

8. Police probationer training in race relations. Peter Southgate. 1982.

9. The police response to calls from the public. Paul Ekblom and Kevin Heal. 1982.

10. City centre crime: a situational approach to prevention. Malcolm Ramsay. 1982.

11. Burglary in schools: the prospects for prevention. Tim Hope. 1982.

12. Fine enforcement. Paul Softley and David Moxon. 1982.

13. Vietnamese refugees. Peter Jones. 1982.

14. Community resources for victims of crime. Karen Williams. 1983.

15. The use, effectiveness and impact of police stop and search powers. Carole Willis. 1983.

16. Acquittal rates. Sid Butler. 1983.

17. Criminal justice comparisons: the case of Scotland and England and Wales. Lorna J. F. Smith. 1983.

18. Time taken to deal with juveniles under criminal proceedings. Catherine Frankenburg and Roger Tarling. 1983.

19. Civilian review of complaints against the police: a survey of the United States literature. David C. Brown. 1983.

20. Police action on motoring offences. David Riley. 1983.

21. Diverting drunks from the criminal justice system. Sue Kingsley and George Mair. 1983.

22. The staff resource implications of an independent prosecution system. Peter R. Jones. 1983.

23. Reducing the prison population: an exploratory study in Hampshire. David Smith, Bill Sheppard, George Mair, Karen Williams. 1984.

24. Criminal justice system model: magistrates' courts sub-model. Susan Rice. 1984.

25. Measures of police effectiveness and efficiency. Ian Sinclair and Clive Miller. 1984.

26. Punishment practice by prison Boards of Visitors. Susan Iles, Adrienne Connors, Chris May, Joy Mott. 1984.

27. Reparation, conciliation and mediation: current projects and plans in England and Wales. Tony Marshall. 1984.

28. Magistrates' domestic courts: new perspectives. Tony Marshall (editor). 1984.

29. Racism awareness training for the police. Peter Southgate. 1984.

30. Community constables: a study of a policing initiative. David Brown and Susan Iles. 1985.

31. Recruiting volunteers. Hilary Jackson. 1985.

32. Juvenile sentencing: is there a tariff? David Moxon, Peter Jones, Roger Tarling. 1985.

33. Bringing people together: mediation and reparation projects in Great Britain. Tony Marshall and Martin Walpole. 1985.

34. Remands in the absence of the accused. Chris May. 1985.

35. Modelling the criminal justice system. Patricia M Morgan. 1985.

36. The criminal justice system model: the flow model. Hugh Pullinger. 1986.

37. Burglary: police actions and victim views. John Burrows. 1986.

38. Unlocking community resources: four experimental government small grants schemes. Hilary Jackson. 1986.

39. The cost of discriminating: a review of the literature. Shirley Dex. 1986.

40. Waiting for Crown Court trial: the remand population. Rachel Pearce. 1987.

41. Children's evidence: the need for corroboration. Carol Hedderman. 1987.

42. A preliminary study of victim offender mediation and reparation schemes in England and Wales. Gwynn Davis, Jacky Boucherat, David Watson, Adrian Thatcher (Consultant). 1987.

43. Explaining fear of crime: evidence from the 1984 British Crime Survey. Michael Maxfield. 1987.

44. Judgements of crime seriousness: evidence from the 1984 British Crime Survey. Ken Pease. 1988.

45. Waiting time on the day in magistrates' courts: a review of case listings practises. David Moxon and Roger Tarling (editors). 1988.

46. Bail and probation work: the ILPS temporary bail action project. George Mair. 1988.

47. Police work and manpower allocation. Roger Tarling. 1988.

48. Computers in the courtroom. Carol Hedderman. 1988.

49. Data interchange between magistrates' courts and other agencies. Carol Hedderman. 1988.

50. Bail and probation work II: the use of London probation/bail hostels for bailees. Helen Lewis and George Mair. 1989.

51. The role and function of police community liaison officers. Susan V Phillips and Raymond Cochrane. 1989.

52. Insuring against burglary losses. Helen Lewis. 1989.

53. Remand decisions in Brighton and Bournemouth. Patricia Morgan and Rachel Pearce. 1989.

54. Racially motivated incidents reported to the police. Jayne Seagrave. 1989.

55. Review of research on re-offending of mentally disordered offenders. David J. Murray. 1990.

56. Risk prediction and probation: papers from a Research and Planning Unit workshop. George Mair (editor). 1990.

57. Household fires: findings from the British Crime Survey 1988. Chris May. 1990.

58. Home Office funding of victim support schemes - money well spent? Justin Russell. 1990.

59. Unit fines: experiments in four courts. David Moxon, Mike Sutton and Carol Hedderman. 1990.

60. Deductions from benefit for fine default. David Moxon, Carol Hedderman and Mike Sutton. 1990.

61. Monitoring time limits on custodial remands. Paul F. Henderson. 1991.

62. Remands in custody for up to 28 days: the experiments. Paul F. Henderson and Patricia Morgan. 1991.

63. Parenthood training for young offenders: an evaluation of courses in Young Offender Institutions. Diane Caddle. 1991.

64. The multi-agency approach in practice: the North Plaistow racial harassment project. William Saulsbury and Benjamin Bowling. 1991.

65. Offending while on bail: a survey of recent studies. Patricia M. Morgan. 1992.

66. Juveniles sentenced for serious offences: a comparison of regimes in Young Offender Institutions and Local Authority Community Homes. John Ditchfield and Liza Catan. 1992.

67. The management and deployment of police armed response vehicles. Peter Southgate. 1992.

68. Using psychometric personality tests in the selection of firearms officers. Catriona Mirrlees-Black. 1992.

69. Bail information schemes: practice and effect. Charles Lloyd. 1992.

70. Crack and cocaine in England and Wales. Joy Mott (editor). 1992

71. Rape: from recording to conviction. Sharon Grace, Charles Lloyd and Lorna J.F. Smith. 1992.

72. The National Probation Survey 1990. Chris May. 1993.

73. Public satisfaction with police services. Peter Southgate and Debbie Crisp. 1993.

74. Disqualification from driving: an effective penalty?. Catriona Mirrlees-Black. 1993.

75. Detention under the Prevention of Terrorism (Temporary Provisions) Act 1989: Access to legal advice and outside contact. David Brown. 1993.

76. Panel assessment schemes for mentally disordered offenders. Carol Hedderman. 1993.

77. Cash-limiting the probation service: a case study in resource allocation. Simon Field and Mike Hough. 1993.

78. The probation response to drug misuse. Claire Nee and Rae Sibbitt. 1993.

79. Approval of rifle and target shooting clubs: the effects of the new and revised criteria. John Martin Corkery. 1993.

80. The long-term needs of victims: A review of the literature. Tim Newburn. 1993.

81. The welfare needs of unconvicted prisoners. Diane Caddle and Sheila White. 1994.

82. Racially motivated crime: a British Crime Survey analysis. Natalie Aye Maung and Catriona Mirrlees-Black. 1994.

83. Mathematical models for forecasting Passport demand. Andy Jones and John MacLeod. 1994.

84. The theft of firearms. John Corkery. 1994.

85. Equal opportunities and the Fire Service. Tom Bucke. 1994.

Research Findings

(These are summaries of reports and are also available from the Information Section)

1. Magistrates' court or Crown Court? Mode of trial decisions and their impact on sentencing. Carol Hedderman and David Moxon. 1992.

2. Surveying crime: findings from the 1992 British Crime Survey. Pat Mayhew and Natalie Aye Maung. 1992.

3. Car Theft: the offenders's perspective: Claire Nee. 1993.

4. The National Prison survey 1991: main findings. Roy Walmsley, Liz Howard and Sheila White. 1993.

5. Changing the Code: Police detention under the revised PACE codes of practice. David Brown, Tom Ellis and Karen Larcombe. 1993.

6. Rifle and pistol target shooting clubs: The effects of new approval criteria. John M Corkery. 1993.

7. Self-reported drug misuse in England and Wales. Main findings from the 1992 British Crime Survey. Joy Mott and Catriona Mirrlees-Black. 1993.

8. Findings from the International Crime Survey. Pat Mayhew. 1994.

9. Fear of Crime: Findings from the 1992 British Crime Survey. Catriona Mirrlees-Black and Natalie Aye Maung. 1994.

10. Does the Criminal Justice system treat men and women differently? Carol Hedderman and Mike Hough. 1994.

11. Participation in Neighbourhood Watch: Findings from the 1992 British Crime Survey. Lizanne Dowds and Pat Mayhew. 1994.

12. Not published yet.

13. Equal opportunities and the Fire Service. Tom Bucke. 1994.

14. Trends in Crime: Findings from the 1994 British Crime Survey. Pat Mayhew, Catriona Mirrlees-Black and Natalie Aye Maung. 1994.

Research Bulletin (available from the Information Section)

The Research Bulletin is published twice a year and consists mainly of short articles relating to projects which are part of the Home Office Research and Planning Unit's research programme.

Occasional Papers

(These can be purchased from the main Home Office Library Publications Unit, 50 Queen Anne's Gate, London SWIH 9AT. Telephone 071-273 2302 for information on price and availability. Those marked with an asterisk are out of print.)

*The 'watchdog' role of Boards of Visitors. Mike Maguire and Jon Vagg. 1984.

Shared working between Prison and Probation Officers. Norman Jepson and Kenneth Elliot. 1985.

After-care Services for Released Prisoners: A Review of the Literature. Kevin Haines. 1990.

*Arts in Prisons: towards a sense of achievement. Anne Peaker and Jill Vincent. 1990.

Pornography: impacts and influences. Dennis Howitt and Guy Cumberbatch. 1990.

*An evaluation of the live link for child witnesses. Graham Davies and Elizabeth Noon. 1991.

Mentally disordered prisoners. John Gunn, Tony Maden and Mark Swinton. 1991.

Coping with a crisis: the introduction of three and two in a cell. T G Weiler. 1992.

Psychiatric Assessment at the Magistrates' Court. Philip Joseph. 1992.

Measurement of caseload weightings in magistrates' courts. Richard J Gadsden and Graham J Worsdale. 1992.

The CDE of scheduling in magistrates' courts. John W Raine and Michael J Willson. 1992.

Employment opportunities for offenders. David Downes. 1993.

Sex offenders: a framework for the evaluation of community-based treatment. Mary Barker and Rod Morgan. 1993.

Suicide attempts and self-injury in male prisons. Alison Liebling and Helen Krarup. 1993.

Measurement of caseload weightings associated with the Children's Act. Richard J Gadsden and Graham J Worsdale. 1994. (available from the RPU Information Section).

Managing difficult prisoners: The Lincoln and Hull special units.

Professor Keith Bottomley, Professor Norman Jepson, Mr Kenneth Elliott and Dr Jeremy Coid. 1994 (available from RPU Information Section).

The Nacro diversion iniative for mentally disturbed offenders: an account and an evaluation. Home Office, NACRO and Mental Health Foundation (available from Information Section).

Other Publications by members of RPU (available from HMSO)

Designing out crime. R. V. G. Clarke and P. Mayhew (editors). 1980. viii + 186pp. (0 11 340732 7).

Policing today. Kevin Heal, Roger Tarling and John Burrows (editors). v + 181pp. (0 11 340800 5).

Managing criminal justice: a collection of papers. David Moxon (editor). 1985. vi + 222pp. (0 11 340811 0).

Situational crime prevention: from theory into practice. Kevin Heal and Gloria Laycock (editors). 1986. vii + 166pp. (0 11 340826 9)

Communities and crime reduction. Tim Hope and Margaret Shaw (editors). 1988. vii + 311pp. (11 340892 7).

New directions in police training. Peter Southgate (editor). 1988. xi + 256pp (11 340889 7).

Crime and Accountability: Victim/Offender Mediation in Practice. Tony F Marshall and Susan Merry. 1990. xii + 262. (0 11 340973 7).

Community Work and the Probation Service. Paul Henderson and Sarah del Tufo. 1991. vi + 120. (0 11 341004 2).

Part Time Punishment? George Mair. 1991. 258 pp. (0 11 340981 8).

Analysing Offending. Data, Models and Interpretations. Roger Tarling. 1993. viii + 203. (0 11 341080 8).

Printed in the United Kingdom for HMSO
Dd297390 12/94 C10 G3397 10170